Making a Deal with Your Bank

Disclaimer

Making a Deal with Your Bank

An Insider's Guide to Managing Your Mortgage Debt

Fran Dalton

ORPEN PRESS

Orpen Press
Lonsdale House
Avoca Avenue
Blackrock
Co. Dublin
Ireland

e-mail: info@orpenpress.com
www.orpenpress.com

Paperback ISBN 978-1-871305-99-9
ePub ISBN 978-1-909518-28-5
Kindle ISBN 978-1-909518-27-8

Printed in the UK by TJ International Ltd

To my wife, Geraldine, and my son, Michael.

About the Author

Fran Dalton is a graduate in Economics from University College Dublin and Fellow of the Association of Certified Accountants. He is also a graduate of the Marketing Institute of Ireland and holds a diploma in Financial Advice (QFA) from the Irish Institute of Bankers. Fran has 35 years' experience in financial services and over that period has assisted many people in achieving their financial plans. His experience spans personal clients, small and medium businesses and corporate entities.

In this book, Fran, a qualified executive coach and trainer, is seeking to make clear the solutions available to people who are in serious personal debt and, in particular, those people with unsustainable mortgage debt.

With an interest in financial education, Fran believes it is now imperative that people become more informed of how financial matters impact their lives. The changing employment landscape, with jobs becoming less secure and retirement benefits being reassessed, means that creating an adequate financial future must form a large part of people's lives.

In this book Fran seeks to clearly explain the options open to those with unsustainable mortgage debt so they can start to look at how they may deal with their situation. Whilst engaging a financial adviser to assist them will more than likely achieve the best result, Fran encourages people not to leave the matter purely to their advisers but to become informed and stay in control of the process. Hopefully this book is a first step in that education and will encourage people to move forward with confidence to achieve an acceptable result.

Fran is a native of Dublin and is married with one son.

www.francisdalton.com

Acknowledgements

This book is not the book I originally set out to write, but the emerging crisis in personal debt made me change course, as I felt there was a need for a consolidation of thinking across all the solutions to the personal debt crisis.

I must acknowledge that the motivation to write this book was prompted to a great extent by the comprehensive press commentary and analysis surrounding the banking crisis and subsequent banking bailouts. The impact on people's lives is being well covered in all newspapers, and I found myself being drawn to the debate. Accordingly I must acknowledge the commentaries and discussion in all the major newspapers which provided food for thought as I tried to formulate this book.

I would like to acknowledge the support and advice provided by my publishers, Orpen Press, and thank them for being so enthusiastic about the book from the beginning. Special thanks also go to my editor, Jane Rogers, for her improvements to the script.

You cannot achieve knowledge in isolation so it is important to thank my many colleagues in banking who assisted me in framing my thoughts, even though at times they have been unwitting participants in framing my views. Their enlightened responses to my clarifications surrounding the mortgage arrears processes are much appreciated.

Finally, I appreciate the support of my wife, Geraldine, in reviewing each chapter before it went to edit.

ACKNOWLEDGEMENTS

Table of Contents

Table of Contents

Table of Contents

Table of Contents

Preface

It's not your ability to take the punches that defines your character. It's your ability to take the punches and keep moving forward.

Rocky Balboa, character in *Rocky*, created by Sylvester Stallone

There is a championship contest coming and it involves you. You're probably feeling anxious, stressed and worried as you consider the strength of the opposition – a seasoned pro with substantial financial muscle, studied responses and well-rehearsed moves. Their punch is formidable but – for now – restrained.

You may be tempted to go into the ring unprepared and short of match fitness. You will throw a few weak punches, fall to the floor and return to your corner. After consoling yourself that you did your best against insurmountable odds, you give up. But in this contest not being match fit is not an option – neither is giving up. Your success or failure will determine the financial future for you and your dependants.

In your corner you also have formidable firepower: the people who developed the championship rules; those who are prepared to coach you; and a referee who may be the final judge. But they are not in the ring – you are. And it is how well you have prepared that will decide whether you win, lose or draw. To be fair to your opponent, they may secretly prefer to have a stronger challenger; a robust exchange might achieve a better result in the long term than a quick knockout.

The championship I refer to is the resolution of the mortgage arrears and personal debt crisis that is having an impact on the lives of so many of our citizens and will place a drag on any economic recovery. The dilemma facing us was outlined concisely by the Governor of the Central Bank of Ireland in his speech to the Limerick Law Society on 14 March 2012:

> For the private sector, the debt burdening many firms and families, who have got caught up in unaffordable levels of debt, hampers their ability – and even, in some cases, motivation – to resume their economic role in society at full potential.

So there is a link between the mortgage arrears problem that faces the economy and the prospect of a financial recovery for the country.

In response to the crisis, our Central Bank has introduced a code to be followed by your lender when dealing with mortgage arrears in relation to a person's primary residence. This is called the Mortgage Arrears Resolution Process (MARP). It outlines the process that lenders should follow with customers who are in difficulties with their mortgage.

MARP will be discussed at greater length in Part II of this book, but at this point it is worth noting that if your difficulties are properly managed, with full engagement with your lender, I estimate that you will gain up to two years, and possibly more, before your worst fears can be realised. This provides plenty of time to achieve an acceptable solution with your lender and perhaps get your life back on track.

Significant support has been provided to those in difficulty on the private residence front, and this will ensure that the sale of these properties will be slow – if they are sold at all. However, this support does not immediately address the issue of personal debt and its negative impact on emotional well-being or on the ability of many people to get back to a reasonably acceptable lifestyle. This may be addressed by the new insolvency legislation, but, again, this will take time. Based on current estimates of the number of people who will take the insolvency route, it is clear that many people will have to resolve their situation by direct negotiation with their lender.

Despite the processes provided to deal with the personal debt crisis there is a sense of a lack of sufficient progress by the banks in dealing with the problem, particularly for home-owners with unsustainable mortgages. In response to this the Central Bank is now seeking real delivery from the banks on this critical issue of mortgage arrears and will introduce specific targets which the banks must adhere to or suffer sanctions which may result in them having to raise new capital. It is envisaged that these specific performance targets for banks will ensure borrowers in arrears will be put on more sustainable solutions tailored to their individual situation. The banks for their part have indicated that some of the MARP terms have impeded their ability to deal with mortgage arrears, in particular those terms concerning customer contact and engagement. The Central Bank has issued a consultation paper on possible adjustments to MARP and is inviting responses from interested parties by 11 April 2013. Following this consultation period some alterations are likely.

A document, entitled Review of the Code of Conduct on Mortgage Arrears, which deals with the proposed changes is available on the Central Bank's website. A significant proposed change focuses on encouraging customer co-operation and engagement with their lender, and if this is not forthcoming the proposed change will make it easier for the lender to proceed to repossession. The objective of the consultation paper is to update the mortgage arrears process so that it continues to provide protection to customers who co-operate with their lender while facilitating and promoting the resolution of arrears cases. This may mean a tougher approach towards those who do not co-operate. As I stress throughout this book, those who fully engage with the process stand to gain from it and will have less to fear from any changes. The consultation process will also consider whether there is merit in allowing a lender to move a borrower in arrears off a tracker rate, where the lender has offered an alternative arrangement which is advantageous to the borrower in the long term. Arrangements involving debt forgiveness may be one example but, again, the criteria seem to be that it must be advantageous and agreeable to the borrower.

This new dynamic being injected into the process has its positives and negatives. On the positive side it puts pressure on your lender to make a deal; however, the pressure to hit the targets may lead to 'one-size-fits-all' type solutions. Your requirement is unique, so you must know what fits you. On the negative side once the push for solutions kicks off, if you are not informed and have not done your homework you may accept a deal which looks good now but is not a good long-term solution. This new target-based approach is welcome, but those people who are best informed and know what they need to achieve may fair best. The framework applies to ACC, AIB, Bank of Ireland, KBC Bank, permanent tsb and Ulster Bank. It applies to both principal dwelling homes and buy-to-let mortgages. If your lender is other than these banks they may have a different approach.

This book is a guide to help you deal with a worrying and traumatic situation. I am confident that it will help you to deal better with your own situation or, if you yourself are not directly affected, to help friends, relations or loved ones through a difficult period.

You will probably need professional help to resolve your situation, but this book will help you understand the processes, provide you with the confidence to address the situation and give you plenty to consider as to how you might resolve it. It explains, briefly and with as little jargon as possible, the various processes that have been put in place to help you.

You should inform yourself about the rules of the negotiations with your lender that will play out in the coming months and years. A mentor of mine once pointed out to me that in business, as in any organisation, you need to 'play the game by the rules' in order to achieve your objective. I was asked to imagine going into a rugby match and playing by the rules of GAA; it was rightly suggested that if I did that I would more than likely end up in the sin bin. Knowing the rules and what impact they can have on you, and realising that achieving your goal can take time and patience, will help you get the result you need.

Unless your problem is temporary and you can see light at the end of the tunnel, you would be well advised to seek professional help. However, even if you do seek professional assistance, you should remain in control of the resolution to your problem, as you will have to live with it for many years to come. Making your own assessment of the outcome you want, and remaining active in the process, can help reduce stress and make it easier to get to the right deal with your bank.

When I tell you that I am a former banker, who spent over 30 years lending to individuals, small and medium-sized businesses, and large corporate entities, you may wonder why I have written this book. Well, I still consider myself a banker, so this is not an anti-bank book. In fact, as I will argue when we discuss the longer-term solutions to mortgage arrears being considered by banks, I believe this approach will yield the best results, if managed properly. I also believe that the more informed both parties to a negotiation are, the better the result.

The world has changed dramatically in the last number of years and what was considered normal some years back is now very far from normal. The work environment is much less secure, job stability is a thing of the past, and wages and salaries are either falling or remaining stagnant. Retirement planning is now being left to the employee as businesses jettison defined benefit pension schemes in favour of the more predictable cost of defined contributions. Many people have not provided adequately for retirement, which some commentators consider another emerging crisis.

All of which means that we all need to increase our knowledge of financial matters and how they impact on our lives. In the new environment you will have to make your own financial future and, in a sense, this book is part of that education. That is why I would encourage you not just to look at your current financial situation in terms of staying in your home, but also to take the long view to ensure that any solution is adequate for your long-term future. In doing this I will be drawing on my interest in lifelong learning, which has taken me from my early studies of economics at University College Dublin through academic studies in accountancy, marketing, banking and personal finance.

Over my career I have gained an understanding of how increasing your knowledge can set you on the path to success. In life in general, those who know most about how the system works, or have the resources to hire professionals who can help them, fare better and achieve more. This is not to say that they do not deserve what they achieve, only to reiterate the old adage that information is power. This book will provide a low-cost entry point to resolving your difficulty and, perhaps, help level the playing field a little for those who do not know how to approach the solution to their personal debt and mortgage arrears difficulties.

The taxpayer has, through various austerity measures, recapitalised some lenders to allow for debt forgiveness, and these lenders have been entrusted with distinguishing between those who can pay their mortgage commitments and those who cannot. This will result in a robust interaction, which you should be prepared for. In fairness, it is not as easy as it seems for the banks to decide who deserves help, and the taxpayer is not in the mood to provide more funds if they are too generous. As I will demonstrate in this book, many possible solutions may defer your problem rather than solve it, and you have to be able to recognise when this is the case before agreeing to any proposal. Some people will achieve what they deserve, and others may even get more than they deserve, yet other people will struggle on and not get anything.

It is rather like going out for a meal with a number of friends who decide to split the bill at the end of the evening. If you are a non-drinking vegetarian you may end up paying more for your meal than the person who has had a fillet steak, a nice French wine and the cheese board. The point is that there is a pot of funds available to resolve your financial problem, but it is limited. If you are a deserving case you need to consider your options. The lenders, for their part, need to get innovative, avoid letting cases 'go legal' and work with those deserving cases to ease the burden through sensible debt deferment, interest forgiveness and, ultimately in some cases, debt forgiveness.

Talking to people about financial matters tends to induce a 'glazed eyes' reaction, so I am hoping that by setting out this book as simply as possible, with as little jargon as the subject allows, will encourage you to read it through. To make it even more accessible, I have dealt with most of the content through a series of questions you may want to have answered. I also provide examples based on fictitious people and situations to explain some points. For those who want an even quicker read, there are summaries and key points at the end of each chapter.

Of course, this book simply could not deal with your individual problem, so please seek advice from a qualified professional before taking any action. What the book *can* do is introduce you to the processes that are available to assist you with your difficulties and to enhance your financial knowledge. It may also be of interest to people who are looking to enter the property market to purchase a family home, or small business owners who are seeking finance. It will go some way to explaining the changing dynamic that has risen from the new codes and legislation.

The various codes and legislative changes are, in a sense, retrospective, as they are designed to resolve a problem that has already occurred, at a time when the rules of engagement between lenders and borrowers were different. The codes that are now designed to keep people in their homes will impact on the lenders' view of mortgage lending in the future.

As a result of the changed employment market, the call for more stringent analysis of mortgage loans and a Code of Conduct on Mortgage Arrears that makes realisation of security more difficult, many potential borrowers may find it more difficult to get mortgages in the future. At the very least, mortgage conditions may be more onerous.

The same may be true for many small businesses, which traditionally relied on the provision of guarantees or the equity value in homes and property to attract bank support. The new codes, insolvency legislation and bankruptcy laws will dilute the value of these supports to a lender and may have an impact on the level of facilities they are willing to lend. This may only be a short-term issue, and over the next number of years lenders may have to develop new lending models to cope with the changed environment while at the same time dealing with the legacy of the boom years.

These issues are not your concern. Neither are promissory notes, Troika reports, fiscal cliffs and all the other issues raised in the media that serve to distract people with debt problems from their primary goal: you need to focus on your challenge, your match fitness, your game plan and your solution.

I hope that this book will help you on your journey to resolve your particular situation.

Fran Dalton

Introduction

What great thing would you attempt if you knew you could not fail?
Robert H. Schuller, US author and motivational speaker

As I mentioned in the preface, I still consider myself a banker, and I have some knowledge of how debt default is resolved. Here's the first insight of this book. If you remember this, it will immediately ease your mind:

> The last thing a lender wants is your house.

You may think this strange, but at this time most lenders will do almost anything to avoid taking your house. If you do nothing more than accept this fact and read no further in this book, you have a good chance of achieving your goal.

The second thing to bear in mind is that lenders have engaged in loan modifications since banking began. Loans go wrong, and lenders have to take a pragmatic approach to resolve the problem. True, the problem is bigger now – but some banks have been capitalised to take care of this.

One slight difficulty is that, as the taxpayer has injected funds into these lenders, there are more calls for a general-ised approach, more commentary and more input from the media and other parties about what the banks should do. In the past, loan modifications would have been done in private and would have been less likely to lead to more widespread loan modifications. Banks prefer to work on a case-by-case basis and in complete secrecy.

The third thing to be aware of is that there are very few house repossessions in Ireland (and very few bankruptcies), and lenders usually only use them as a last resort. This does not mean that the lenders are pushovers, and it may be that the level of repossessions and bankruptcies will increase in the coming years, but it does mean that lenders will not rush to repossess unless they see no other option. This may provide the latitude for you to do a reasonable deal.

To give you an idea of whether (and how) this book can help you, below is an outline of the topics we will be discussing in the following chapters. This will give you an idea of how you can use the information in this book to achieve what you need in relation to managing your mortgage debt. Reading the book will help you become more informed about areas that, until now, you may have found worrying or confusing. As I mentioned in the preface, this is not an anti-bank book, so I will not be passing on any tricks or schemes to avoid what you legitimately owe and can afford to pay. But for those who need help, an understanding of the processes available to provide that assistance is essential.

The book is divided into four parts, and each part deals with a specific area.

Part I

Part I will give you an overview of the processes in place to help you manage your mortgage debt.

It will also answer many of the questions you might have, questions such as, 'Which processes provide the best chance of debt forgiveness?' and, 'What is the impact of each on my standard of living or my ability to stay in my home?' These will be addressed initially in Chapter 1 and dealt with in more detail in later chapters.

Chapter 2 briefly describes the market participants; the role of the Central Bank; and the lenders, financial advisers and others you may come across as you seek to deal with your current situation. This is important because there is a lot of noise out there from advisers wanting to help resolve your problem and from the media updating you on every move by the lenders, the government and other authorities. While you may be having problems, remember that this is a lucrative market for others; so knowing how each group fits into the equation is of paramount importance. Chapter 2 also provides a cautionary note in relation to picking the right adviser.

Chapter 3 gives an insight into how lenders generally deal with loan or mortgage defaults. This chapter will be of particular interest to those with buy-to-let mortgages or excessive personal debt, which fall outside the new process designed to assist those whose problems relate to their family home.

Chapter 4 outlines how to manage the negotiation with your lender. There are key negotiation skills you need to know about, and even if you decide to use a professional adviser, you will need to stay active in your case and understand the negotiation process. We will first bring you through the principles of negotiation so that you know how to think about and approach this stage of the process. Negotiations have a formula, and you need to know this and be prepared to last the course. How many times have you seen labour or legal disputes resolved at the eleventh hour? Negotiations take time, as people tend to hold out and need to exhaust all the options so that they feel happy that doing the deal is the best result possible. This takes time, and if you give up, get angry or fail to plan adequately you will lose out. Once you grasp the theory and practice of negotiation we will look at what you can do, based on your financial position, to construct your case to the bank.

Part II

Now that you are familiar with the overall process and have begun to see how it could be of use to you, Part II will get into the specifics of the Mortgage Arrears Resolution Process (MARP). This was the first process set up by the Central Bank of Ireland to deal with mortgage arrears. Its aim is to assist those who are in difficulty with mortgage arrears on their private residence.

The solutions set up by MARP consist of mainly short-term modifications to your mortgage loan, such as an 'interest-only' period when interest is paid and capital payments are deferred. You will be unlikely to achieve either interest or debt forgiveness under the MARP process, so if this is what you need you should look at the other solutions discussed later in the book.

As I will show you in Chapter 5, the key to using MARP effectively is to engage with the process in order to get the protection that MARP offers. It is also important to know what is required of you and the bank on an ongoing basis. Operating within the process successfully will buy you plenty of time to consider your choices and the best way to get your life back on track. Knowledge of the process will also be important to get whatever concessions are needed to achieve your goal in relation to the resolution of your mortgage problem. Chapter 5 provides a general introduction, and in Chapter 6 we discuss the communication process that you will start with your lender, and how to set the agenda from the beginning to achieve your desired result.

Perhaps the most important chapter in this book in terms of achieving interest or debt forgiveness is Chapter 7, in which I work with you on assessing your current financial position. This is the cornerstone of everything you hope to achieve – an accurate assessment will make the solution to your problem much clearer. Many people just focus on the immediate problem – paying a contribution to their mortgage so that they can stay in their home – and stop there. Chapter 7 will help you to realise that staying in your house will probably not be a major difficulty, but finding a long-term, acceptable solution to your problem will be harder, and this should be your focus.

The final chapter in Part II, Chapter 8, deals with how your lender will assess your case, your right to appeal any negative response from your lender, and what options you have if you do not achieve your goal at this point.

Part III

In this part of the book I look at the longer-term solutions now being used by lenders and discuss the situation for those who have difficulty with properties not covered under MARP. People not covered by MARP – those in the investment property market or the buy-to-let market – are people whose intention in buying the property was to rent it out to achieve a better return. If your problem property is not your private residence but an investment property, MARP is not directly intended to help you. In addition, the Central Bank of Ireland is encouraging banks to take a proactive approach to dealing with problem buy-to-let mortgages in arrears. The positive aspect of this is that there may be an opportunity to achieve some debt relief. However, if your private residence is not in difficulty this will require strong negotiation, as some of the solutions may require an attachment to this property.

The longer-term strategies now being operated by lenders are referred to as the Mortgage Arrears Resolution Strategy, or MARS. It is understood that many people require a more permanent solution to their situation, and an element of debt deferment may be necessary. I say debt *deferment* as there is no automatic interest or debt forgiveness under MARS, so to achieve this requires careful negotiation.

The key to any negotiation with the bank is making an accurate assessment of your current financial position and your future income-generating prospects. You will also need to realistically assess your goals and incorporate these into any proposal you make to your lender. Even if you use a financial adviser to help you, which is recommended, you will have to prepare this information for the proposal to your lender. As I will repeat many times throughout this book, being informed about the process and knowing what you want to achieve will give you more control and less anxiety over the outcome.

One point to note for those with buy-to-let mortgages is to examine carefully who is liable on the loan and factor this into any deal you strike. It is almost always the case that your spouse or partner will be in the family home, but it may not always be the case that your spouse or partner is liable on other commitments such as investment property or personal debt. Bringing them into the solution could worsen their financial position without improving yours, so if this is the case you may need to achieve a trade-off.

Part IV

In Part IV we will look at the new legislation enacted to deal with the high level of personal debt in the country, which is seen as restricting our ability to generate growth and employment due to weak consumer demand. This new legislation involves brand new laws to tackle personal insolvency without the need for bankruptcy, and some amendments to the bankruptcy laws that make this option less stark.

A key point about insolvency is that it does not mean you have to prove that you will be insolvent for the rest of your life. Many people consider themselves solvent, as they believe they can resolve their financial situation over their lifetime. In fact, the new insolvency legislation takes a short-term, five-year view. You need to be insolvent at present but also have a personal insolvency practitioner certify that you are likely to remain that way for the next five years. This is a key requirement of being able to avail of the new insolvency solutions to resolve your financial difficulty with your lender.

Your lender is still actively involved at this stage, as the insolvency legislation is a non-judicial (non-court-based) process. It involves you appointing a personal insolvency practitioner to make a deal with your lenders on your behalf. As the process is, in effect, a bargain struck between you and your lenders it does not have the ramifications of bankruptcy, so you will more than likely stay in your home and, if your employment contract allows it, stay in your job. The process also provides for a reasonable standard of living for you and your family with the possibility of significant debt forgiveness after six or seven years. It sounds good, but there's a catch, and that is that your lenders have a major say or (as some would contend) a veto on whether you achieve this. But this is not entirely true, as I will show in this part of the book. Chapters 12 to 14 cover the three processes set up to deal with personal insolvency: Debt Relief Notices (DRNs) for smaller debt, Debt Settlement Arrangements (DSAs) for unsecured debt, and Personal Insolvency Arrangements (PIAs) for those with secured debt up to €3,000,000.

In Chapter 15 we explore the new amendments to the Bankruptcy Act. The law relating to bankruptcy has been viewed as draconian – people had to wait twelve years to be released from the process and were subject to many restrictions on building a new life. The significant change is that this period has now been reduced to three years, and the amendments also accommodate a reasonable standard of living while you are in the bankruptcy process. Bankruptcy is not a decision that can be taken lightly, as it involves the sale of all your assets, including, in most cases, your home. Professional help is needed, but the change in legislation makes it an option worth considering for individuals whose ability to earn a living is unaffected by the bankruptcy process and also for people in general when constructing a proposal for their lender. Professionals who are debarred from practising their profession if made bankrupt may find this option closed to them.

Summary

Achieving the right result in your interaction with your lender may involve travelling a very long road, with rest stops along the way. These rest stops are vital to your success, as they will dictate whether you accept the deal on the table or move on to a new process. MARP has seven possible outcomes, and MARS has three possible outcomes. Add to this the three procedures under the insolvency legislation and the final bankruptcy procedure and you have fourteen possible solutions. If you factor in possible combined solutions the numbers get more complex, so you have to stay alert and be active in the solution to your financial difficulty.

Using the process correctly will allow you time to consider options, but at the core of the process is the decision about how you and your lender will deal with the position you are in. You need to be active in this process. Ignoring the situation or leaving it to others may increase the stress associated with it and may lead to a less than optimal result.

My feeling is that you will need professional help if your difficulties cannot be solved in the short term. If you move to the insolvency process, professional presentation is mandatory, so it makes sense to seek it earlier – at the MARS stage, when long-term solutions are being discussed. Many people feel they do not have the money to pay for professional advice. However, as I will stress when we discuss the assessment of your financial position, you need to factor in this expense when preparing your budget for your lender.

While many people are in difficulty, current estimates are that only between six and ten thousand of us will avail of the options provided by the new insolvency legislation. Most other people will have to deal directly with their lenders to achieve an acceptable result, and the outcomes will be hard fought by lenders. There is much talk in the media about debt forgiveness, but, at the same time, there is no plan for a general, across-the-board programme of debt forgiveness for those in difficulty. Your lender will work on what they call a case-by-case basis, which means individual negotiation, though they may have some generalised formulae with which to work. These could be specific to the bank or follow some general market principles.

That's why having an understanding of the negotiation processes and where you stand to benefit within them is vital to your success. You must convince your lender that their best option is the option you propose, and that this is one you can live up to. All the processes leading up to bankruptcy have a strong emphasis on keeping you in your home, but the fear of losing your home can cloud your judgement and weaken your chances of achieving the best solution.

Selling your house may also be your best option, and you need to consider it. Remember, lenders want to reduce their loans, so by selling you help them with this, and if they have already impaired your loan (this is a nice way of saying that they have written off part of it against profits) they may be willing to do a deal on the residual debt. I appreciate that this means you will have no home, but renting may prove more economical in the medium term, depending on the size of your loan. In addition, the location of your property may not now suit your changed circumstances, and this could be a good time to offload it.

We will end this introduction with a quote from the speech by the Governor of the Central Bank of Ireland to Limerick Law Society on 14 March 2012:

Step-by-step the challenges of this crisis of over indebtedness will be overcome, and it is crucial that, in the process, the fabric of Irish society and the contractual underpinnings of our economy are protected. Thus, fairness is a key objective, which means both that debtors who can afford to pay do pay *and* that efficient and effective arrangements for ensuring that those who cannot now pay fully are given a clear and coherent path forward that is consistent with affordability and sustainability.

There is much to consider in this statement, and it reinforces the principle that those who can pay should pay. It also places a big responsibility on lenders to manage the process to ensure that only genuine cases get relief. This is not as easy as it seems, as many people will look for interest and debt forgiveness. If you are a deserving case it is your responsibility to inform yourself and make your case to your lender. It is unlikely that they will automatically grant you relief if you do not ask for it and prove that you need it.

The mechanism is now in place to assist you, so do not waste the opportunity to seek help – if that is what you need.

Part I

Managing Your Mortgage Debt: An Overview

Part I will outline the processes put in place to deal with the mortgage arrears and personal debt difficulties now facing our economy. It will also introduce the key market participants who will assist you. It will give an insight into how lenders approach dealing with loans in default and finish with some guidance on managing the negotiation with your lender to make the deal.

1

Processes for Dealing with Mortgage Arrears and Personal Debt

Knowledge is an antidote to fear.
**Ralph Waldo Emerson, US essayist, lecturer and poet who led
the Transcendentalist movement of the
mid-nineteenth century**

Property is in our DNA: but is it time to consider new DNA? Property ownership in Ireland is among the highest in Europe. Is it time to reconsider our attitude to property ownership, particularly for those in negative equity who may be able to avail of the remedies now afforded by the new debt resolution processes?

We are a nation of homeowners: citizens in other countries are happy to rent. We prefer to own our home and pay it off over our working life, spending thousands on its upkeep, taxes and insurance. Many of us refurbish and extend our homes beyond our real requirements.

Many people who are now in negative equity will spend the best part of their lives repaying a mortgage on a home they or their children may never own and spend thousands on a property that may end up belonging to someone else.

This is because many of the loan modification solutions being offered to those with personal debt difficulties see people merely as tenants in their house. Many people could have as much debt owed on their home when the loan matures as they have at present.

Case Study

John and Alison have a €400,000 mortgage on a property valued at €200,000. Their financial situation has deteriorated in recent years, and they anticipate that their income into the future will be roughly 70 per cent of past annual earnings. They are unable to meet their current mortgage payments.

They have been offered a *split mortgage* by their lender. This means that their mortgage is split into two loans, a Loan A and a Loan B, as follows:

- Loan A: €250,000, which they can continue to pay over 25 years
- Loan B: €150,000, which will be 'warehoused' for the present, but will still accrue interest (say 4 per cent annually)

If John and Alison pay off their Loan A mortgage in the 25 years, their position will be as follows:

- Remaining Loan B Mortgage: €150,000 @ 4% for 25 years = €400,000
- Estimated value of property (assume 2% annual growth) = €328,000

If John and Alison fail to make inroads into paying off Loan B during the 25 years, they will still be in negative equity thereafter.

Should the property increase in value at a higher rate, they may have equity in their home.

John and Alison need to consider the following:

- Is it likely that the value of their property will increase by 100 per cent to clear Loan B?

- How will they be able to pay off Loan B at retirement age?
- If they cannot repay Loan B, what is their lender's expectation of repayment?
- What is their expectation of their ability to service an extended loan at retirement?
- Can they negotiate a zero interest rate on Loan B to ease the financial burden in 25 years?
- Are there other options to consider? Insolvency? Or even bankruptcy?
- Do they need professional advice?

John and Alison's case is not necessarily the same for everybody, but it highlights the hard bargaining that will be a feature of unravelling the personal debt burden in the country.

Is Your Home an Asset?

Some financial experts would argue that your private residence should not be considered an asset, as it is unlikely that you will sell your home at a future date to liquidate funds. You may, of course, view it as a financial buffer for use in dire financial need or to fund nursing care in old age. However, a house is normally passed on to family, who may use it as equity to get them started in life or to fund leisure pursuits.

So, apart from the enjoyment you get from knowing that you are living in your own home and, perhaps, the pleasure you receive from passing on the house to your children, a house may be a burden rather than an asset at this time, particularly if you are in severe negative equity.

I am mentioning this up front and before discussing the various mortgage resolution processes because the sale of your house may be an option worth considering. This is because, in the pursuit of loan modification or debt forgiveness with your lender, an arrangement that involves selling your home could very likely achieve the best outcome.

Your lender will typically prefer debt forgiveness solutions to be accompanied with a reduction in their loan book and, given the current bank credit environment, your ability to refinance your reduced loan may be limited. Holding on to the loan and forgiving part of the debt is not an attractive solution for your lender. Your lender's opening position is likely to be an element of loan modification, while keeping you fully liable for the debt.

The sale of the property provides an opportunity for reward to you, as the loan is being reduced, and a settlement on the residual debt on favourable terms may be possible.

Case Study (Continued)

John and Alison decide that the split mortgage is not attractive. The monthly repayment on the €250,000 Loan A is €1,320 per month and for this they could rent a perfectly good house in a desirable area.

If the house is sold they will have residual debt of €200,000 (house sold for €200,000). They decide to offer the bank €100,000 over ten years, based on support and guarantees from their family.

Will the lender accept this solution to close out the loan? If the lender refuses, could they use the insolvency legislation to get an even better result?

As we will see when we look at the new insolvency legislation, the residual debt could be considered unsecured debt, and if John and Alison have other unsecured borrowings it may dilute their lender's control over the repayment outcome.

If John and Alison's lender agrees to their proposal, the next ten years will be financially tight. However, John and Alison will know that the end is in sight. Any loan resolution process should ensure that you do not end up a slave to a loan for the rest of your life and still have the burden of a mortgage when you are in your seventies.

The example above raises the question of whether life could be better if you sought a deal under which the house is sold. More important, it will make you think hard about any loan modification proposal that may be offered by your lender. To ensure that it is acceptable, it is necessary to seek an incentive or reward for a new proposal, particularly if the new arrangement is going to seriously affect the standard of living you will have in the future.

Later in the book we will look at the wider aspects of your financial future, such as educating your children and having a comfortable retirement. This will help you think about what is best in the long term.

If I sell and do not fully repay, will I ever get finance again?

You may be concerned that a debt forgiveness solution will prevent you getting bank finance in the future. When you apply for a loan with a lender they will normally require a credit check. If you had late payments on other loans or a loan modification with another lender it could show up on this check and will need to be explained. If you enter an insolvency arrangement you will appear on the register that the Insolvency Service of Ireland keeps of all those who have entered such an arrangement. If you arrange an adjustment to your mortgage under the mortgage resolution process it will also be recorded on your credit history.

Any new lender will take the circumstances of your case into consideration. However, you can be sure that banks will tend to be more stringent in their assessment in the future. Given that your credit history is already affected, you will have to consider whether a solution that does not involve debt forgiveness is better for your credit rating in the long term.

Given the current state of the economy and the problems the banks are dealing with, it could be a number of years before credit flows freely again. Other sources of credit exist to deal with the shortage of bank credit. You may have seen the increasing trend for car manufacturers to provide the credit required to buy their vehicles. This is an area of finance once occupied by the banks. Economies of scale dictate that car volumes must be produced and, as car finance is required, the car manufacturers come up with their own solutions when bank finance is scarce.

Banks are in the business of lending money and will in time adapt to the changed circumstances and find ways to lend money, even to those with poor credit rating due specifically to the property bust.

Is everybody in with a chance of debt forgiveness?

As I mentioned in the introduction, there is no general scheme to provide for debt forgiveness. There is no debt forgiveness calculator where you can enter in all the assets that you have – property, shares, house contents, etc. – and come up with an estimate of your gross wealth; no calculator into which you enter all the loans you have, such as your mortgage, loans on investment properties, car loans, credit card and other debts; and no calculator where you enter your income and prospective earnings. You can't do all this and then estimate how much debt forgiveness is available to you and collect a cheque to give to your lender. No such calculator exists.

Any decision as to whether you achieve debt forgiveness will be based on the assets and liabilities mentioned above and your income, but only after a negotiated interaction between you and your lender. There are two clear principles that run throughout the various processes set up to deal with the burden of personal debt:

- Those who can pay should pay.
- Those who cannot pay deserve help.

The fear of a general scheme is embodied in the term *moral hazard*. This idea creates a concern that a process that makes it easy for people to avoid debts will be used by some people to do so. This could lead to more losses than anticipated in the banking system and, perhaps, more money being required from the taxpayer. The process also seeks to ensure fairness for citizens who did not extend themselves on buying property during the boom: they should not have to support to an unfair degree the resolution of the problem.

While most people may not be very happy with having to provide – through the austerity measures that have been introduced in the last few years – the solution to our personal debt crisis, they realise that if a solution is not found, it may be difficult to return the economy to the growth levels needed to generate employment.

Under Starter's Orders!

The funds to solve the problem have been set aside, and the process to manage the negotiations is in place. The question is, are you ready? Have you considered your case for interest relief or debt forgiveness?

We know all the big picture reasons for the process – the IMF plan, the regeneration of the economy – but these need not be your immediate concern. You may be tempted to just let things drift and take whatever solution your lender offers as long as you can get by. That is not a good idea, for a number of reasons:

- The economy will eventually improve, and solving problems may become less urgent.

- You may miss the opportunity to place your finances on a footing that will give you a comfortable life, before and after retirement.
- Despite the fear of moral hazard, those who are best informed about the process and can use their knowledge to present their case will benefit.
- The taxpayer has provided funds to solve this problem. If you genuinely deserve to partake in the process, you should.

Debt Forgiveness Will Be a Lucrative Business

Before we outline all the players in the market who have a part in the process designed to relieve mortgage debt, it is worth mentioning that in the next 12 to 24 months you will be bombarded with offers to help you solve your personal debt problem. Advertisements claiming up to 75 per cent off personal debt as achievable are already appearing. The intensity of these adverts and approaches will increase. Just like the mania that surrounded property, there could be similar excitement about debt relief. While in the past banks could provide debt relief and the deal would remain confidential, it is difficult to imagine that all deals done under the current process will be kept private. The public interest in property, debt relief and the banks means that in the coming years the media may feature reports about deals done. People were attracted into property during the boom years based on available money, attractive advertising and the promise of success. They may also have been influenced by families' and friends' stories of 'no-brainer' investment opportunities. The herd mentality was everywhere.

The same could easily happen with debt relief – individuals with little knowledge of the process could be attracted to a fee-paying situation with a financial expert who guarantees to handle matters. While this may be what is required to resolve your case, it is important that you do your own research and assessment to ensure that you get the right advice, at the right price, which achieves the right result for you. This book can help, but the responsibility to be informed is yours.

What are the processes of debt relief and debt forgiveness?

I will provide a summary of all the processes set up to resolve the mortgage arrears problem and the wider personal debt problem in the economy. The journey from start to finish is a marathon, not a sprint, and you should prepare yourself for the long haul.

You may be anxious to finalise matters, but doing it quickly at the expense of an unworkable deal does not make sense. I recommend expert advice from the start, combined with keeping yourself informed and active in the resolution of your difficulty.

The processes of debt relief and debt forgiveness fall into four categories or levels, outlined as follows:

Processes of Debt Relief and Debt Forgiveness

Mortgage Arrears and/or Personal Debt Process	Codes or Laws Guiding the Process
Level 1: Mortgage Arrears Resolution Process (MARP) This consists mainly of a short-term loan modification and adjustment that provides cash-flow relief until the seriousness of the situation is assessed. There is generally no talk of debt forgiveness at this stage.	*Code of Conduct on Mortgage Arrears 2010* This code is issued under Section 117 of the Central Bank Act 1989. The code sets out how banks should deal with customers who are in arrears or are likely to go into arrears on their family home. The emphasis is on helping people work through their prob-lem and remain in their home.

(Continued)

Processes of Debt Relief and Debt Forgiveness (*Continued*)

Mortgage Arrears and/or Personal Debt Process	Codes or Laws Guiding the Process
Level 2: Mortgage Arrears Resolution Strategy (MARS) This level (which is a subsection of MARP above) is designed for more long-term solutions to mortgage arrears where it is assessed that you are unlikely to be able to pay the current mortgage payment amount. There is still no talk of debt forgiveness, and it seems the intention is that you remain liable for all the debt – in other words, this is debt deferral rather than debt forgiveness. Debt forgiveness or interest relief may be possible. This will require negotiation as part of the formal structure that Level 2 provides.	*Bank response to Central Bank request* This second level of the mortgage arrears resolution process is provided by your lender at the request of the Central Bank of Ireland to address the long-term needs of those in difficulty. It is recognised that some people may be unable in the near future to service the mortgage they originally entered into. In many cases the problem could be that repayment as originally envisaged is impossible.
Level 3: Personal Insolvency Arrangements (PIAs) This involves using a personal insolvency practitioner, who negotiates debt relief or forgiveness on your behalf. The process seeks to achieve some form of debt forgiveness as an alternative to the deferred solutions in Level 2 or bankruptcy at Level 4.	*Personal insolvency legislation set up by the government* The process does not involve the courts directly (it's a non-judicial process) and provides for an agreement to be reached between a borrower and his/her creditors using a personal insolvency practitioner as an intermediary.

(*Continued*)

Processes of Debt Relief and Debt Forgiveness (*Continued*)

Mortgage Arrears and/or Personal Debt Process	Codes or Laws Guiding the Process
Your personal insolvency practitioner, once they establish that you are eligible for a PIA, seeks to negotiate with your lenders and other creditors on your behalf to agree on a new proposal to deal with your debts. The agreement, if approved, will run for six to seven years, after which you will be free from unsecured debts. Secured debt remains in place, but the objective is to reduce it to a level in line with your ability to repay.	There are eligibility conditions, and the process is monitored and overviewed by the Insolvency Service of Ireland and the court to ensure that all conditions are met. There is an emphasis on keeping you in your home, and it seems that you will be able to continue in your current job if your employment contract allows this. To achieve the benefit of a PIA you must get the agreement of your lenders. Some commentators believe they have an effective veto on the process.
Level 4: Bankruptcy This involves an application to the court by you or one of your creditors. This involves the sale of all your assets for the benefit of your creditors. It will normally involve the sale of your home.	*Irish Government Courts: Bankruptcy Acts 1988* This is a judicial (court-based) process whereby a court-appointed official assignee oversees the sale of all your assets for the benefit of and distribution to your creditors.

Case Study

Paul and Mary have a mortgage of €150,000 from their lender. Paul has lost his job but is hopeful that he will return to work within the next six months.

The loan has fifteen years to run, with monthly payments of €1,100: €500 in interest and €600 in capital repayments.

Paul and Mary approach their lender for a loan modification, but are happy that they can at least meet the interest payment of €500.

A Level 1 solution would involve a short-term loan modification, which, after looking at all the options, may consist of one of the following:

- Paul and Mary pay €500 (interest only) per month for a period.
- Based on an assessment of Paul and Mary's financial position, their lender may seek a contribution of between €0 and €600 towards capital repayments as well as the €500 interest payment.

When Paul returns to full-time employment the monthly payment will increase to allow for the deferral of the capital repayments during the loan modification period. If Paul and Mary were on interest-only payments for one year (€500 per month), their monthly repayments would increase by approximately €60 per month. This is not an extra charge but reflects the fact that the capital is now being repaid over a shorter period.

There is no debt forgiveness involved at this level and the amount owed remains the same.

At what level do I receive debt forgiveness?

As we shall see when we look at your personal financial position, it is essential that you make an *accurate* assessment of your financial position now and into the future. Achieving debt forgiveness is not automatic and is unlikely to be offered to you by your lender. You can place it on the agenda from Level 1, but remember that any assessment by your lender as to whether to offer debt forgiveness as part of their solution will be based on your financial situation.

While the processes outlined above are to a certain extent separate, you may, when preparing your case, be better prepared if you treat them as one. This is because you may have to proceed from Level 1 to Level 4 to achieve your result. Alternatively, if you have decided that Level 4 is not an option it will make your preparation for Levels 2 and 3 more important, as your negotiation position may be weakened if you wish to avoid bankruptcy

We will cover each level in more detail later in the book, but rather than keep you in suspense, here's a summary of debt forgiveness at each level:

Level 1

Level 1 provides short-term relief until a clearer picture is available to your lender regarding your long-term ability to repay your mortgage. Level 1 is focused mainly on your private residential property. Given the difficulties of untangling a mortgage on buy-to-let properties from your family home, these will also tend to be dealt with by your lender, at least initially, in a similar fashion. Short-term Level 1 solutions include the following:

- Only interest is paid on your mortgage for an agreed period.
- Interest plus some capital is paid, but not the full capital due under the mortgage.
- You make no payments for a period of time (a moratorium on payments).
- You extend the term of the mortgage to reduce payments. This can be used where you can afford the new extended monthly payment amount and can pay off the mortgage over a reasonable time, say by age 65.
- The type of the mortgage could be changed, except in the case of tracker mortgages.
- Arrears and interest could be added to the loan.
- A combination of any of the above.

As you can see, these solutions provide temporary relief, but the amount of your liability remains the same or could increase if you cannot pay the full interest due every month. There is no debt forgiveness anticipated at this level.

The Level 1 solutions can suit those borrowers whose difficulty is temporary and who can see their way to financial recovery and repayment of the loan amount.

Level 2

Level 2 provides long-term solutions for those with mortgage arrears and repayment difficulties. They comprise three main options:

* A trade-down mortgage
* A split mortgage
* A mortgage-to-rent scheme

Debt forgiveness is not automatic in these options, particularly with split mortgages and trade-down mortgages, where the main benefits are affordability of the new mortgage and the ability to stay in the family home. However, you retain full liability for the original amount borrowed. You need to consider whether a solution at this level is acceptable to your long-term financial position.

Warehousing – or putting some of the debt to one side until some future date – does not get rid of it. You still owe the money. If you have no chance or only a very slim prospect of being able to pay the debt in the future, you need to consider carefully what you agree to. (We will cover these options in more detail in Part III.)

Level 3

It is only at this level, where you are considering the personal insolvency route, that debt forgiveness is clearly on the agenda and is, in fact, the object of the exercise. For this process it is mandatory to engage the services of a personal insolvency practitioner to represent you to your lenders. Their objective is to convince your lender to provide debt forgiveness and to persuade them that the solution offered is preferable to you looking to the Level 4 bankruptcy solution.

This will not be simple, because the voting rights afforded each class of lender means that you must convince the majority of them to agree. There is more detail on this process in Part IV.

Level 4

This is the final option, and it involves either you or your lender seeking your bankruptcy. In the past this was quite a long-drawn-out solution, as it involved twelve years in the hands of a court-appointed official assignee, but the term has now been reduced to three years. Bankruptcy places many restrictions during its term on the person made bankrupt. The most significant thing is that it involves the sale of all assets. We will look at this in Chapter 15.

Do I get to stay in my home?

All processes, except bankruptcy, place an emphasis on you being able to remain in your family home. It is more than likely that you will be able to do so. Level 1 and 2 solutions, which are covered by the Code of Conduct on Mortgage Arrears, focus strongly on you remaining in your home. As pointed out, the solution they offer involves deferring debt and interest payments rather than debt forgiveness. In other words, you stay in your home and keep the same level of debt. If you are heavily in debt or insolvent you may need to get debt forgiveness on the agenda at Level 1 and 2 or consider options that involve the sale of your home.

Even at Level 3 the insolvency legislation states that any proposal prepared by your personal insolvency practitioner should aim at not requiring you to sell your home, subject to certain tests that will be considered by your personal insolvency practitioner. These include:

- The cost of remaining in the home (including rent, mortgage loan repayments, insurance, management fees, taxes, etc.)
- Your income and other financial circumstances as disclosed in your financial statement
- Your reasonable living and accommodation needs
- The cost of staying in your home versus living in alternative accommodation

The point here is that while it is not certain that you will be able to stay in your home under a Personal Insolvency Arrangement (PIA), the legislation does allow for considering and analysing the possibility. It may come down to the appropriateness of the house to family size and income, and the solution may involve still having a family home, but not the one you are currently living in – in other words, trading down to a smaller house.

Will I have enough to live on?

Here again the insolvency legislation provides assistance. It specifies that any PIA should not require you to make payments to your lenders that do not allow you to have sufficient income to maintain a reasonable standard of living for you and your dependants. It will be up to the Insolvency Service to provide guidance on what is a reasonable standard of living.

Currently at Levels 1 and 2 you will complete a standard financial statement outlining your assets, liabilities, income and outgoings. Your lender will seek to restrict outgoings so that you can at least pay interest and perhaps some capital.

Accordingly, there is no set formula. It may well be the case that when guidance is provided on what a reasonable standard of living is, it will be adopted across the financial sector.

However, it is quite possible that setting a reasonable standard of living will be problematic. Different social groups have different expectations about living standards. They also have different expectations about lifestyle and accommodation. Will a reasonable standard of living be set in relation to your past income or living standards, or will it be a 'one-size-fits-all' estimate? At the moment we do not know: we will have to wait for the guidance provided by the Insolvency Service.

SUMMARY

After reading this chapter you will realise that getting some loan modification or relief will not prove that difficult as the codes and legislation implemented by the Central Bank of Ireland and the government place a strong emphasis on keeping people in their homes. Your lifestyle will be monitored and, at best, you will have a reasonable living standard. (However, this depends on what 'reasonable' means to you.)

Debt forgiveness can only be assured at Level 4 – bankruptcy. However, it should be possible at Level 3 – insolvency. It is also possible at Level 2, but you will have to make strong, rational and effective arguments to your lender that will convince them that some level of debt forgiveness is the best outcome. Setting out and analysing your financial position is of utmost importance: it is the cornerstone of all negotiations.

Key Points in this Chapter

1. There are a number of processes in place to help you achieve a modification to your mortgage and other loans.
2. There is also an expectation that you will engage fully with your lenders in seeking a solution. In fact this engagement has to last at least six months before you apply for a PIA.
3. The objective of PIAs and bankruptcy is debt forgiveness.
4. The mortgage arrears process is initially focused on solutions that defer liability rather than forgive liability. However, debt forgiveness may be achieved based on strength of argument.
5. All processes, except bankruptcy, emphasise you being able to remain in your family home.
6. A key driver of your success will be your financial statement, which will be forensically examined by your lenders. You must get this correct. (We will discuss this in greater detail in Chapter 7.)
7. It is important that you take the long view and consider that a better result may be achieved by selling your home.
8. The Level 1 and 2 mortgage arrears process can last a lifetime with annual reviews, so if you cannot envisage a way out of your financial difficulties in five years, it may be worth taking advice on other solutions.
9. All solutions will provide for a reasonable standard of living and, while you may not be happy with the proposed lifestyle, in the case of Level 3 and 4 resolutions it will not last forever.
10. The taxpayer has provided for debt forgiveness to fellow citizens. This is an opportunity for those in most need to get their lives back. Do not waste it.

2

The Market Participants

*People create their own success by learning what they
need to learn and then by practising it until they become
proficient at it.*
Brian Tracy, Canadian author and motivational speaker

Now that you may have an idea of the four processes put in
place to assist with the personal debt crisis in this country,
this chapter will outline the various players you may encoun-
ter on your journey to resolve your mortgage debt situation.
It will also deal with some other questions you may have
about the timing of each process, debt forgiveness, your
lender's ability to veto your proposals, and how you prove
insolvency.

The Participants in the Market

We have provided an overview of the various processes that
have been put in place to help you deal with your lender
on your financial position. The legislation enacted by the
government will also assist this process and will introduce
a new government body, the Insolvency Service of Ireland,
and a new style of professional adviser called a personal
insolvency practitioner.

In this section we'll look briefly at some of the participants
you may come across:

- Central Bank of Ireland
- The banks
- Financial Services Ombudsman
- Money Advice and Budgeting Service (MABS)
- Personal insolvency practitioners
- Insolvency Service of Ireland

The Central Bank of Ireland

The Central Bank Reform Act 2010 created a new single unitary body – the Central Bank of Ireland – responsible for both central banking and financial regulation. The new structure replaced the previous related entities, the Central Bank and the Financial Services Authority of Ireland and the Financial Regulator. The Act commenced on 1 October 2010.

The Central Bank seeks to achieve the twin and related objectives of a stable financial system and consumer protection.

From a consumer protection point of view the Central Bank of Ireland has issued a number of codes on how institutions should deal with their customers and prospective customers. All these codes are available to download from the Central Bank of Ireland website (www.centralbank.ie). The key codes for our purposes are:

- **Consumer Protection Code** (2012) – Provides direction to regulated entities such as lenders as to how they should deal with their customers. This code, being a general code, may be of particular interest to those whose financial difficulties are not specifically addressed by another code.
- **Code of Conduct on Mortgage Arrears** – The key regulatory code for dealing with the growing mortgage arrears problem and how lenders should address this with their customers. We will go into some detail on this code, as it is the basis of the Level 1 and 2 arrears processes already outlined in Chapter 1. I shall focus on what I consider to be the most important elements in helping you resolve your financial situation.

- **Code of Conduct for Business Lending to Small and Medium Sized Enterprises** (2012) – Provides direction on lending to the SME sector. This code could be of interest to those with property difficulties in their personal name, which qualifies as a business lending.

The Central Bank of Ireland has many other functions, which are outlined on its website, but we will focus on the codes listed above to assist you in your dealings with your lender.

The Banks

The challenge for those seeking relief from their financial difficulties will be to negotiate effectively with their lender to achieve a deal that is acceptable and maintainable. Your lender will be guided by the various codes and legislation put in place to which they must adhere. They will be reluctant to concede ground unless your argument is convincing and they have no better solution on the table. Doing your homework and getting good advice will give you the best chance of success.

Financial Services Ombudsman

This is a statutory body set up to deal independently with unresolved complaints you may have in relation to your dealings with your financial service provider. The Financial Services Ombudsman's Bureau is an investigative service only. It is not in a position to offer advice or information regarding the details of your complaint/query, as it must remain impartial at all times.

Money Advice and Budgeting Service (MABS)

This is a free, confidential, independent service for people in Ireland who are in debt or in danger of getting into debt.

MABS will work with you and provide support in drawing up realistic budgets and maximising your income. MABS also supports clients in dealing with their debts according to their budget.

If you have multiple lenders and different types of debt (personal loans, credit cards, etc.) MABS can help you propose a solution to your lenders.

Personal Insolvency Practitioners

Recent personal insolvency legislation represents a radical overhaul and modernisation of the country's personal insolvency law. The process of personal insolvency will be described more fully later in this book. However, it is important to recognise the three parties that make up this process:

- Personal insolvency practitioners
- The Insolvency Service of Ireland
- The court

The process is non-judicial, which means that while the court confirms the arrangement and provides initial protection to you if you enter the process, it does not adjudicate on any proposed arrangement between you and your lender. The deal is negotiated between the personal insolvency practitioner you appoint and your lender. It is a requirement of the legislation that you appoint a personal insolvency practitioner – under the insolvency process you cannot deal directly with your lenders or other creditors.

There are two main requirements for using this route to solve your financial difficulties:

- You must be insolvent. This will involve producing a prescribed financial statement.
- There is a maximum of €3 million on secured debt.

There are many other conditions, and your personal insolvency practitioner will cover these with you, but their first objective is to establish whether you are eligible.

Accordingly, if you are seeking a long-term solution, before starting any negotiations with your lender it may be best to have an initial meeting with a personal insolvency practitioner to ensure that you are eligible to take this course of action. If negotiations with your lender are not getting the required result it would be useful to know whether personal insolvency is an option.

In general, having an adviser at an early stage can focus the discussion with your lender for the benefit of both of you, and this is worth considering.

If, following an unsuccessful negotiation with your lenders, you decide that insolvency is the best course of action, you will be unable to engage directly with your lenders under the personal insolvency process, and you must work through a personal insolvency practitioner.

Personal insolvency practitioners have many duties to carry out in order to achieve a successful result. They will explain the process and its implications for you, and advise you on the possible outcomes.

Once you decide to proceed, in the first instance:

- They can get you protection from your creditors/lenders for a period of 70 days (it may be possible to extend this by 40 days). This is called a protective certificate.
- During this protection period they will try to achieve an agreed solution to your debt problem, which will more than likely involve debt forgiveness.
- They will deal with the Insolvency Service of Ireland in relation to their requirements.

The personal insolvency practitioner will first require a financial statement of assets, liabilities and expenditure so that they can assess your eligibility for a PIA. A PIA is a plan, agreed with all your creditors, for how you will deal with your debt problems.

Based on the criteria set out in the legislation and your prescribed financial statement they will apply to the Insolvency Service for a protection certificate.

There are many practitioners who can assist with personal insolvency, and the number is likely to increase. As personal insolvency is not a judicial process, many professionals can get involved in this work. There may be a new form of registration or authorisation for this role – as is the case with financial advisers – and it is important that you work with someone who is authorised and qualified to represent you.

Insolvency Service of Ireland

This new body will carry out a number of functions under the new insolvency legislation. The functions likely to be of most interest to you are:

- Monitoring the operation of arrangements relating to personal insolvency
- Processing applications for protective certificates
- Maintaining a number of registers for protective certificates, Debt Relief Notices (DRNs), Debt Settlement Arrangements (DSAs) and PIAs
- Contributing to the development of policy in the area of personal insolvency

Finding an Approach to Your Difficulties

You will have realised by now that the process of achieving anything other than some short-term relief from your financial difficulties may be a long one. Your lender will more than likely opt for an extended period of consultation with an emphasis on deferring any talk of debt forgiveness until it is absolutely necessary. They will need to distinguish between those who can pay and those who can't. They will also be seeking to structure deals that recover the maximum amount of capital, either now or in the future. You must also bear in mind that the extent of mortgage arrears in the banking system will slow progress on individual cases unless you seek to drive the agenda yourself.

If I were to estimate how long the process would take, I would say that it could take between 12 and 36 months to complete all stages. This is based on the fact that before you enter the Level 3 (insolvency) process it is expected that you will have spent at least six months trying to resolve the situation with your lender. The insolvency process can take a further 110 days. Therefore, even if you have a plan to resolve your position as quickly as possible it will be almost a year before you have to decide on whether to go for bankruptcy.

Proper engagement during the earlier stages of the mortgage arrears process could see you spend at least twelve to eighteen months in discussion with your lender before any major action takes place.

One of the difficulties with the mortgage arrears process for those who are seeking a quick result, including debt forgiveness, is that it can drag on for some time. This may suit some people who only require short-term assistance. However, these early processes do not automatically result in debt forgiveness, and if debt forgiveness is your goal you need to drive it yourself and keep it on the agenda. The Level 2 Mortgage Arrears Resolution Strategy (MARS) was devised for longer-term solutions. However, as I pointed out in Chapter 1, MARS is primarily focused on debt deferment rather than debt forgiveness.

You must control your own destiny if you are to achieve the result appropriate for you. For this reason it is worth spending time getting informed about the process and considering your initial view on what you can achieve before engaging professional help. As I will continue to remind you, it is your responsibility to secure your financial future. Professional advisers can help, but you will be expected to adhere to any revised deal they negotiate for you with your lender. In the case of personal insolvency, if you breach the deal you can end up back where you started with all your original debts.

Some of the key issues you will need to get straight in your mind before entering into extensive talks with your lender are:

- What is your current and prospective financial position? Are you insolvent with no prospect of reversing this situation in the next five years?
- How does your current indebtedness affect your ability and that of your dependants to have an acceptable financial future?
- What is your attitude to selling your home or other properties to achieve the desired result?
- What do you consider to be your best result?
- What is your goal? Debt forgiveness? A better living standard? Or both?

You need to involve and get the opinions of all those affected by your current financial position, including your spouse or partner, adult children and guarantors.

We shall address these issues throughout the book, but it is important to start thinking about them now.

How long will it all take, and what can I expect?

Mortgage Arrears Timeline and Outcomes

	Duration of the Process	Likely Outcomes
Mortgage Arrears Process (MARP and MARS)	• Initial period: 12–24 months • Long-term deal may involve servicing an element of the loan with a deferment of a portion • Continuous annual review of financial position with a view to enhanced payments • Process ends when the mortgage returns to capital and interest repayments *or* the loan is repaid *or* the property is sold • Sale of the property may require a deal to be reached on residual debt (if any) • Process likely to continue for many years	• Low possibility of debt forgiveness • Possibility of interest forgiveness • You may be liable for the full amount of the loan and interest. • In the most difficult case you may never own your home. • You will have continued financial austerity with annual monitoring of your income. • You get to stay in your home.

(*Continued*)

Mortgage Arrears Timeline and Outcomes (*Continued*)

	Duration of the Process	Likely Outcomes
PIA	• Negotiated solution, which could be completed in 6–7 years (subject to conditions)	• Element of debt forgiveness • Possible to stay in home • Reasonable living standard during the process • Can expect improved standard of living after 6–7 years
Bankruptcy	• Court-based solution • You could be out of bankruptcy in 3 years.	• Safest to assume all assets will be sold, including the family home • Reasonable standard of living for 3 years • Can expect improved standard of living after 3 years • Debt free after 3 years

Personal insolvency looks like the best deal for debt forgiveness… Is it?

Insolvency is not bankruptcy, and it does not have the same impact on your lifestyle or impose restrictions on you being able to work. Insolvency may therefore be of particular benefit to professional people and entrepreneurs, as they may be able to keep working during the insolvency period and leave the process with substantially reduced debt.

Personal insolvency is not a judicial process; it is basically a deal struck between you and your lenders. Should a person become bankrupt, however, it may have an impact on their ability to continue to practise their profession under either their employment contract or the rules of their professional body. It is quite likely that many professional associations would take the view that if the problem is not directly related to the person's professional practice and is non-judicial, continuing to practise is allowable. The difficulty is not related to any professional malpractice on the insolvent person's behalf, but rather to unrelated property transactions.

A business person who is made bankrupt will have restrictions placed on them relating to their participation in any new business venture or management of a company. In insolvency, many of those restrictions may not exist, though raising finance may prove difficult. For those who can generate an income based on their innate or acquired skills and who are not tied to a particular company, the insolvency legislation may prove useful, as they come out of the process after six or seven years.

It seems that any person, even those in paid employment as teachers, civil servants or even bank officials, will be able to enter the insolvency process, achieve debt forgiveness and continue working in their current job (provided their employment contract does not disqualify them). As this is new legislation and is intended to solve a personal debt crisis it would not make sense for those who enter the insolvency process to have their earning potential restricted.

How easy will it be to achieve debt forgiveness if I use the insolvency process?

In order to achieve debt forgiveness you first have to be certified as insolvent and then you have to convince your lender or lenders that you cannot repay your debts in the long term. Furthermore, you have to convince them that your proposed solution is the best that can be achieved and that it is in their interest to agree to it. This will mean that you and your personal insolvency practitioner will have to strike a balance between what you can reasonably afford to pay and what your lenders will receive in bankruptcy.

> *Why would they agree to forgive debt when they can just defer it indefinitely and hope that things improve?*

Your lender will decide on debt forgiveness as part of the solution if it suits their overall approach to dealing with the problem in their loan book. The following are some of the areas or solutions they will consider:

- Your lenders may want to solve the problem and have it disappear. They will not be a pushover, but if you are persistent and come up with a fair proposal they may want to do business.
- You prepare your case well, make a convincing argument and provide an offer that is superior to that which they would achieve via bankruptcy.
- You, having exhausted all the arguments, move to achieve personal insolvency to ensure that your proposal is offered within a formal framework with court oversight. This may provide some protection or a second chance at a PIA (explained below).
- If you are willing to consider bankruptcy as an option and your lender is fully aware of this, it may focus their mind on your solution.

The key is to try to construct a deal that is better than your lender's best alternative so that they can be sure that there is no better option.

Personal Insolvency Is a Formal Process

You cannot just opt for insolvency and achieve it as you might with bankruptcy. While insolvency has the advantages of being less public, less restrictive on your lifestyle and also on your business activities, you need the majority of your lenders to agree, in accordance with a voting structure, to your proposal. This means analysing not only your position but also what your lender's best outcome is if you don't co-operate.

Some would say that the lender has an effective veto on whether you achieve a PIA. However, the process has the benefit of being a formal process with a beginning, a discussion about alternatives, and a definite end date – by which time either a deal is struck or it is not. So there is an eleventh hour, which will focus the minds of all parties. Another advantage is that to enter the process you will have to appoint an insolvency practitioner, who is independent of your lender. If they judge you to be eligible, they will arrange protection from your lenders and other creditors to allow them to sound out with those creditors what is acceptable to them.

The process will culminate in a proposal, which will either be accepted or rejected. However, each creditor will have to consider carefully whether they would do better with bankruptcy. If you have multiple lenders and other creditors, you have a reasonable chance of getting a result.

How does the alleged bank 'veto' work?

Areas in the legislation that seem to favour the lender are the limit on the amount of secured debt with which you can enter insolvency, and the voting threshold you must achieve to get your proposed arrangement agreed.

You must have secured debt of no greater than €3 million to avail of a PIA. Secured debt above this amount is outside the legislation unless all the lenders or other creditors agree to allow it to be included. If you have multiple lenders or creditors, in order to get your proposal agreed you must achieve the assent of 65 per cent of the creditors by value, and half of the secured creditors and half of the unsecured creditors.

So to achieve your goal your proposal and argument must be strong enough to achieve broad agreement and you must provide in your proposal sufficient incentive for each lender to vote in your favour.

Why might the bank go all the way to bankruptcy?

Your lender will want to achieve the best deal, and this is understandable. However, they will always look at the next best alternative to doing a deal with you. They will undertake a robust analysis of your expenses to restrict your outgoings, and you may find this unworkable. However, the guidance on what is a reasonable standard of living, which the Insolvency Service of Ireland will provide, may help you on this (unless you find what they recommend restrictive).

During the insolvency process, it may be difficult for your adviser to put together a solution that involves you remaining in your house, if the lender feels that you have the capacity to trade down and you are resisting this option.

In many cases, a big difficulty, particularly for well-paid individuals, is the fact that once the process ends in six to seven years the lender has no access to your income should it increase beyond its current level. This may result in the lender preferring to look for long-term deals outside the insolvency process that involve a continuing payment over time. This may not be all bad if you can agree payment of a fixed amount for ten to twenty years or until an agreed amount is paid off, and in return you achieve a good lifestyle, stay in your house and get an adequate level of debt forgiveness.

There is a delicate balance here that must be considered, and we will look at it in Chapter 4 when we discuss managing the negotiation to make the deal.

Will an unsuccessful outcome in the personal insolvency process lead to bankruptcy?

Bankruptcy is not a natural progression if the personal insolvency approach fails. You can apply for bankruptcy yourself if this is part of your strategy to resolve your problem. However, your lenders are unlikely to move quickly to this option unless the negotiations are acrimonious or they need to protect their security position. The new insolvency legislation has made changes to the law on bankruptcy that make it less attractive for creditors who seek to make you bankrupt. We will look at bankruptcy in Chapter 15.

But one significant adjustment is that the court, before agreeing to the commencement of the bankruptcy process, will look at whether you and your lenders have adequately sought to resolve the situation through the insolvency process. The court has the power to defer the bankruptcy process and refer the matter back to attempt resolution under the insolvency process.

This is why I mentioned earlier that the insolvency process, being a formal process with an independent practitioner, may provide some protection. Your lender may have to ensure that the deal you offered during the insolvency process was properly considered and that bankruptcy can achieve an enhanced result for them.

Will people know that I have entered into a PIA?

One of the responsibilities of the Insolvency Service, as outlined above, is to keep a register of those who enter a PIA. The public will be able to search the register to check whether people they are about to do business with have entered the process. The legislation also requires you to inform any person from whom you intend to get credit in excess of €1,000 that you have entered a PIA.

How do I prove personal insolvency?

You will have to enlist the assistance of a personal insolvency practitioner, who will help you determine this and, more important, assess your eligibility for a PIA.

Here is a working definition and test of personal insolvency:

> A person is insolvent if they have insufficient assets to pay their debts and financial liabilities.

There are two primary tests for determining insolvency:

1. **The cash flow test** – An individual is regarded as insolvent if they are unable to pay debts as they fall due.
2. **The balance sheet test** – An individual is insolvent if total liabilities outweigh the value of assets.

These will provide a rough guide, but, ultimately, it will be up to your insolvency practitioner to assess whether you are insolvent and to certify this to the Insolvency Service of Ireland.

Whilst the definition above is a commonly held definition for 'insolvency', the Insolvency Act defines insolvent as follows:

> ... insolvent, in relation to a debtor, shall be construed as meaning that the debtor is unable to pay his or her debts in full as they fall due.

This definition seems to confine insolvency to the cash flow test alone. This may mean that those people who are in severe negative equity but can just about manage to pay their debts will be unable to avail of personal insolvency. In their case bankruptcy may be the only option available.

Finally, your insolvency practitioner has to certify that you are likely to remain this way for the next five years. This is significant because many people may look to resolve their problem with their lender over their lifetime and do not see themselves as technically insolvent.

Establishing that you are insolvent early in the process may be useful in your negotiation with your lender, who may suggest a long-term solution without any reward such as debt or interest forgiveness. Being aware of your options under the insolvency process may help you assess alternative outcomes and also whether the deal suggested by your lender is reasonable.

SUMMARY

There are a number of institutions and practitioners you may come across on your journey to rebalance your financial position. The Central Bank of Ireland oversees the initial mortgage arrears process, and the government's insolvency legislation takes over if agreement is not reached at the earlier levels. Bankruptcy is the final option and, like the other options, needs sound analysis and professional advice before you proceed.

With the exception of bankruptcy, there is a strong emphasis in the mortgage arrears and insolvency process on helping you remain in your home or at least having a family home should the one you are living in be deemed excessive for your needs. As a reasonable living standard is also envisaged, ensure that you do the figures accurately to make your case.

It's your responsibility to consider all the options available to you in order to deal with your financial difficulties, and you should not expect your lender to make a proposal for you. An adviser will help, but you should not be passive in the process.

Key Points in this Chapter

1. There are a number of participants in the market. The most relevant to you are probably your lender and (at a later stage) your personal insolvency practitioner.

2. Consider all options available to you to deal with your financial difficulties.

3. Options include MARP, MARS, personal insolvency and bankruptcy.

4. If you feel you have a good case, put debt or interest forgiveness on the agenda early on.

5. Consider whether you are insolvent. A meeting with an insolvency practitioner may be required to confirm this.

6. Staying in your home may not be difficult, but assess the real cost in terms of the overall deal and burden of debt going forward.

7. A reasonable living standard for you and your dependants is factored into the process.

8. Remember, the insolvency and bankruptcy options have a defined timeframe, whereas the lower-level mortgage arrears solutions may go on for your lifetime.

9. Construct a proposal that will be attractive to your lenders and is better than their next best alternative.

10. Use a professional with the right qualifications.

3

Dealing with Default

Insecurity exists in the absence of knowledge.

Anonymous

There is currently a massive emphasis on personal debt levels, prompted in no small way by the IMF's plan for the recovery of the country and repayment of the funds loaned. The huge level of personal debt is a drain on the economic and social health of the country, and if it is not resolved it will be difficult to envisage a return to the favourable economic times we have experienced in the past. Something needed to be done, and though the problem has existed for over four years, we finally have a structure through which the issue of debt forgiveness can be dealt with.

Many people's financial difficulties will be confined to their family home. They may have purchased a house in the boom times which is now in negative equity, and, in addition, their economic circumstances may make them unable to repay the loan as agreed.

For others the problem may be different: it may relate to investment property, either in Ireland or abroad; and yet others may have multiple properties. The provision of interest-only mortgages by lenders during the boom years, combined with falling rents, has resulted in the twin problems of negative equity and a lack of repayment capacity for many borrowers.

The Process Is the Same for Personal and Business Debt

The process for dealing with any debtor experiencing problems repaying a debt is straightforward and broadly similar whether the debt is personal or related to business.

In fact, formal structures, which in most cases involve debt forgiveness, have been in place for many years. Incorporated limited liability companies are viewed in the eyes of the law as separate legal entities (like a separate person) from the people who own them, and it is not uncommon for companies that experience difficulties to enter a legal arrangement that forgives debt. In these arrangements creditors accept debt forgiveness in return for payment of a portion of what is due.

Case Study

Michael is a director and owner of his company, Michael Ltd.

Michael Ltd has significant debt, which, due to poor trading over the last year and the loss of two major contracts to a competitor, has put the company into financial difficulties.

Fortunately for Michael he has not guaranteed the debts of Michael Ltd and he has managed the company properly, with no hint of reckless trading. He now needs to decide what to do.

Michael could seek an informal arrangement with his creditors, which may result in debt forgiveness for the company, thus allowing it to survive and continue trading.

In the eyes of the law Michael Ltd is a separate entity from Michael and, as he has not guaranteed the company debt, he is not liable for the repayment of this debt.

If no agreement can be reached with the company creditors, Michael can place the company into a formal court-based process. If his intention is to continue trading with the business, Michael could opt for *examinership*. Alternatively, if he wants to call it a day and close the business, he could choose *liquidation*. Either option should result in an element of debt forgiveness with no personal impact on Michael.

What is the purpose of the new processes for personal debt?

Just as there are formal processes for company debt, the new structure being put in place by the Central Bank and the Irish government seeks to formalise a method of dealing with personal debt in a streamlined way while at the same time ensuring that those who can afford to repay their debts do so. The processes set up involve a number of checks and balances to try to ensure that only those people who cannot pay their loans get relief.

While the procedures set up to deal with the debt problem as it applies to mortgages on the family home has an emphasis on keeping people in their home, the same emphasis does not apply to investment or buy-to-let mortgages that are in difficulty.

A more robust approach to dealing with buy-to-let properties has been encouraged, and an emphasis on the sale of investment properties in difficulty will be more likely. This approach may have ramifications for your home if it is not in negative equity and is seen by your lender as a source of repayment.

The goal of the process is to deal with problems quickly and provide fair solutions, but there is no plan for general forgiveness of debt, and lenders will deal with problems on a case-by-case basis.

Accordingly, those seeking relief must go through the various stages of the process to achieve this, and the result is not certain. This is why I continue to stress the need for a proper financial assessment, becoming informed about the process and examining all your options, including bankruptcy.

Case Study

Niall is in financial hardship brought about by a buy-to-let property investment and a loss of income. He decides to contact the bank, tell them about his situation and see what they will suggest. Is this the best course of action?

It may be better for Niall to assess his position first so that he has a good handle on the type of outcome that will be right for him and his dependants.

As I have already outlined, and will continue to reinforce throughout the book, you must be prepared for your interaction with your lender. This should be your approach to any difficulty, whether it arises from the family home or a buy-to-let property.

The assessment (which we shall look at in more detail later in the chapter) includes:

1. Doing a full financial assessment using the standard financial statement available to download from your lender's website
2. Completing an accurate family budget
3. Assessing the future prospects for your profession or trade, including earning potential
4. Reviewing insurances, pensions and life cover for you and your dependants

Having completed Steps 1–4, you should then outline your position in writing to the bank and set the agenda for your meeting.

The Standard Process for Dealing with Problem Loans

Normally the process used by your lender for dealing with loans in difficulty will involve five steps. This is similar to the process designed for dealing with mortgage arrears on residential properties that we will deal with in Part II of the book.

Understanding the thinking process and approach of lenders will help both those in difficulty with their family home and also those who are outside the code for mortgage arrears if the property does not qualify as their family home.

Step 1

You acknowledge that you have a problem and let your lender know that there is one. The lender may have already gleaned this from the conduct of your account, but the sooner you advise the lender the better. Lenders do not like surprises, so it is best to let them know in advance that there may be a problem. Ignoring the lender is futile and not to your advantage, and while letting them know is not a case of 'a problem shared is a problem halved', it will at least take a worry off your mind and allow you to focus on the solution.

As I have already stressed, the process set up by the Central Bank and the government has a strong emphasis on keeping you in your home. The arrangements for buy-to-let mortgages are different, but the lender will more than likely follow the same process when dealing with these cases.

Step 2

Having alerted your lender to a possible or actual problem in relation to your loan, you then need to present a proposal to rectify the problem if that is possible. There may be a temporary setback in your finances which, with some forbearance on the part of your lender, will be rectified in the short term. This will more than likely be accommodated by your lender.

If the situation is permanent, this may require a different solution and could involve a discussion concerning the sale of property or other assets.

Step 3

You will now look to negotiate an agreed solution with your lender. The solution will be based on the relative negotiating strengths of both parties: the case you make for continued support, or maybe the incentive or concession granted by your lender for selling the assets in a co-operative way.

Step 4

Your lender will more than likely outline their position on any new arrangement, whether it is continued support, sale of assets or partial debt forgiveness. This may be their final position or there may be an element of flexibility. It will be guided by what negotiators call their next best alternative. For your lender this will follow an assessment of what they will yield in terms of recovery of the debt if they realise their security and pursue you for the residual debt.

As I will explain in Chapter 4 on managing the negotiation to make the deal, the key to success will be your ability to find common ground with your lender and a solution that is the best option for them. When presented with a proposal, any negotiator will look to their next best option or alternative, and if this is significantly less than what is currently on offer, they may agree to the proposal.

Step 5

You will either accept the proposal put forward by your lender as their best position or seek to appeal it in the hope of an improvement and a new agreed solution. In seeking an agreed outcome you should also be aware of what your next best alternative is, which may include personal insolvency or bankruptcy. Where the relationship between you and your lender goes from here will depend on how satisfied each party is with the proposed solution.

Case Study

Tony and Joan, who have secured debt of €1,200,000, have gone through the five steps with their lenders and are unhappy with the result. They have completed an assessment of their financial position, looked at their future prospects and feel that the deal being offered is not reasonable.

What are their options?

- They can look at personal insolvency. Introducing the services of a personal insolvency practitioner will formalise the negotiation with their lender, put their proposal to a vote and – as a precursor to bankruptcy – make the lenders think hard about their proposal.
- If Tony and Joan are unsuccessful in getting their lenders to agree to their proposal, they could consider bankruptcy and the possibility of being free of all debt in three years.
- They could just adopt a 'wait and see' strategy. This is a valid option once you have done your assessment, made a fair proposal and feel you can go no further. The initiative is left with the lender, and if you remain co-operative and stay engaged with the process, the lender may have to change their stance.

From the five steps above you can see that the process for dealing with loans that experience difficulty is quite standard and predictable. For anybody new to this situation it is important that you are aware of the process and know how to use it to achieve your desired outcome.

Stay the Course and Stay Engaged in the Process

After Step 5, if things are not going to plan, you may be tempted to sever the relationship with your lender or even to blame the lender for not providing more assistance or time. You may also view the problem as a shared problem, where the bank automatically takes a financial loss. However, it is important to remain in discussion with your lender. If you stay engaged in the process, it is your lender that will have to make all the moves. This will not only save you money but also keep you in your house longer while the process plays out and you take action to get your finances back on track.

What will my lender think when I inform them of my problem?

From the lender's point of view, late payments on a loan are an irritation, but when a loan seems to be unrecoverable they start to consider their options. When considering the provision of a loan, lenders look at many factors, including the person's track record, employment record and ability to repay.

In general this comes down to two factors, or what is known by lenders as the 'two exits'. The first exit or repayment source for the loan is the borrower's ability to repay from income or cash flow. If this is sufficient the lender will also look to the second exit, which is the value of the security they will hold for the loan.

During the boom years, except when providing a 100 per cent mortgage loan, the lender had a valuation for their security that was in excess of the loan amount. With property prices rising, home loans had a safe lending status. Generally, when it comes to property lending, lenders like to know that in a worst case scenario the sale of the property will redeem the loan.

Lenders have faced large losses on property in the past, but these tended to be on commercial property such as offices, retail outlets and hotels. Waiting for an improvement in a loan situation is something lenders are not programmed to do. There is a saying among senior bankers – 'Your first loss is your least loss' – which basically means that things seldom get better and if you can liquidate your security reasonably quickly it is possibly the best you are going to do.

The scale of the current difficulties makes it difficult to sell property quickly. Our experience with property over the past number of years may not make you sympathise with your lender, but it may provide some understanding of their standard approach.

Later in the book we will consider the alternative solutions available to resolve your financial situation. We will see that a solution that involves selling the property and that gets the property off the lender's balance sheet may stand the best chance of debt forgiveness.

When dealing with your lender, it is likely that you will be negotiating with a different person from the one who lent you the money. The lender will have a specialist team of people who deal with loans that develop problems. In fact, for mortgage arrears on family homes your lender is required to have such a team under the Code of Conduct on Mortgage Arrears introduced by the Central Bank. This specialist team will be instructed on the approach your lender wishes to take in dealing with loans in arrears and what solutions they are willing to offer.

The Central Bank has determined a number of possible short-term solutions or loan modifications, which lenders must discuss with those in mortgage arrears. At the request of the Central Bank, lenders have introduced a number of longer-term solutions to deal with mortgages viewed as unsustainable in the short term. So there are already some sample structures in place, which we will discuss in Parts II and III of this book. If any of these, when presented by your lender, does not fit your particular situation, the challenge for you will be to negotiate suitable adjustments to them that may make them acceptable.

The fact that you will be dealing with a specialist team of loan officers may be of assistance to you, particularly if you can put forward a valid argument for your position. The reason for this is that in many cases the lender will have assessed their best outcome on your loan and have a position on the areas in which it could concede. If you stay with the negotiation and do your homework properly you stand a better chance of achieving your outcome.

What about guarantors on my mortgage? How will they fare?

We saw above that Step 1 in the process is acknowledging the problem and informing the lender. You also need to inform all parties to the mortgage about the difficulties. These may include your spouse or partner, a co-borrower or a guarantor such as a parent or other family member. All parties need to be brought into the solution. While you may be in difficulty and able to avail of the new legislation, they may not. In fact, a guarantor's financial position may be quite strong, and the lender may look to this for support or repayment.

You may be able to avail of the debt forgiveness provisions of the insolvency legislation and achieve some debt forgiveness, but this does not automatically provide the same reduction for a guarantor to your loans. The lender may be forced to accept your insolvency arrangement, but they may still pursue the guarantor. It is best to ensure that all parties to the loan are involved at each step of the process as this provides them with an opportunity to clarify their position and deal with it as part of the discussion with your lender.

SUMMARY

You can take it as read that your lender will not be sending you a letter advising you that they are reducing or forgiving an element of your debt. Despite the fact that they will already have taken a view on the recoverability of your loan and may have provided for this in their accounts, they will still expect full recovery of the loan amount.

They may rely on your sense of pride and your desire not to be seen as a defaulter on your debts. Or they may believe that if they play hardball you will come up with money from some source, such as friends, family or assets that can be sold.

To be fair to the lender, it is very difficult to get an accurate and independent fix on a person's financial position unless they provide full disclosure. While debts can be confirmed using a Credit Bureau check, the full extent of a person's assets can only be established if they disclose them.

Under the mortgage arrears process set up by the Central Bank, which I will deal with later in the book, lenders have been entrusted with assisting those who cannot pay their mortgages and ensuring that those who can pay do pay. This requires your lender to engage in a robust assessment with you. In other words, the lender cannot just accept everything you say at face value, and they will seek to maximise their position. This is their job – and this is how you must view it. *Your* job is to make an effective case to negotiate a deal that is acceptable to you.

While your current circumstances may be difficult, the lender will also be looking to your wider financial prospects, which could, down the road, include repayment sources such as increased job prospects, pension lump sums or inheritances.

Bearing in mind the two sides of this equation – a sceptical lender on one side and a distressed borrower on the other – the stage is set for an interaction which could see both sides win or both sides lose.

Key Points in this Chapter

1. Your lender is not going to take the initiative and provide debt forgiveness. You must drive the process.
2. Your lender will have a standard process for dealing with any loan that incurs difficulties. This process has five steps:
   - i.   Step 1 – Acknowledging the problem and advising your lender
   - ii. Step 2 – Providing financial information, which may achieve temporary assistance
   - iii. Step 3 – Assessing and negotiating a long-term solution

---

iv. Step 4 – A proposal from your lender

v.   Step 5 – You either agree with the lender's solution or you look at alternative options

3. There is a set process for mortgage arrears on family homes, which lenders must follow; and there are designated short-term solutions that must be considered.

4. Lenders also have some longer-term solutions, but these do not automatically involve debt forgiveness.

5. Investment property or buy-to-let loans are not covered by the mortgage arrears process, but lenders will more than likely follow the five steps outlined in this chapter.

6. It is important to remain engaged in the process and carry out your own assessment.

7. Keep all parties, including guarantors, in the loop – they need to protect their position.

8. If your lender makes an offer you cannot live with, consider your next options.

9. Other options include personal insolvency, bankruptcy and 'wait and see'.

4

The Negotiation Process: Doing the Deal

*It is not because things are difficult that we do not dare; it
is because we do not dare that they are difficult.*

Anonymous

Negotiation is sometimes described as an art form, perhaps
in reference to the many moves and counter-moves that form
part of the process. You must see it as such and realise that it
can take some time before both parties (you and your lender)
realise what is in their best interests and make the deal.

Many people feel that they are hopeless at negotiation.
They think of the many times they are outwitted by their
children, family or friends, and talked into doing or providing something they do not initially want to provide. Almost
everyone is a poor negotiator in this situation as there is an
emotional element to the relationship that can undermine
your willpower.

Your approach to your mortgage arrears should be busi-
ness-like. In this chapter I will give you a structure and a
way of thinking about the negotiation. Always keep in mind
when you are negotiating with your lender that whatever
deal you achieve has to be one you can both live with and
stick to. It also has to provide an acceptable life for you and
your dependants.

Starting the Negotiation

You are now aware that certain mortgage arrears processes are focused on modifications to your loan that do not have debt forgiveness in mind. These are what I term the Level 1 (MARP) and Level 2 (MARS) processes. I anticipate that in many cases some level of interest forgiveness is achievable at Level 2 MARS. If you reach this point it is clear that there is no short-term prospect of you being able to repay your mortgage, so interest forgiveness should be one of your goals.

The dilemma for you when offered a long-term solution that provides immediate relief is whether to accept it and hope things improve or whether to resist any offer until you have one that is acceptable. Having completed your financial assessment you will have a good idea what will work for you. If you are uncomfortable with negotiating for yourself it may be best to seek professional help.

The MARS long-term solution offers an opportunity for an acceptable solution for many people in difficulty if some innovation can be brought into it by you and your lender.

Case Study

Peter and Joan's lender has offered them what looks like a great deal, which provides immediate relief from their problem.

They currently have a mortgage of €400,000 on a family home valued at €200,000.

Their financial position has deteriorated to the extent that they can, with tight budgeting, service a mortgage of €250,000. They are worried and would prefer not to lose their home.

Their lender introduces a long-term solution:

- The lender will accept a €250,000 mortgage over 25 years to age 65.

- The balance of the loan (€150,000) will be warehoused for the present.
- Their arrangement will be reviewed annually.

In the example above, Peter and Joan have achieved an immediate solution to their difficulty. However, there are a number of aspects to the deal that may need clarification and negotiation:

- If Peter and Joan work hard and increase their income, what portion of their increased disposable income will their lender expect to go towards the warehoused loan?
- Will the warehoused loan be accruing interest, and at what rate?
- At age 65 when their income reduces, what level of payment will be expected as a portion of income?
- Will they be expected to sell the property if it returns to positive equity and they are not in a position to service the warehoused loan?
- Peter is expecting a lump sum at retirement which he hoped would contribute to improving their lifestyle. What portion of this will their lender expect to be used to pay down debt?
- What is the arrangement if Peter and Joan receive an inheritance or win the lottery?
- When they die, will the lender expect full recovery of the loan including interest?
- Is there any pre-agreed incentive for Peter and Joan to forego current spending to repay the warehoused debt quickly, such as an element of debt forgiveness?

Many of these questions can be negotiated, resolved and recorded with a legal agreement. Peter and Joan will have a clear picture of what is agreed and, as long as they adhere to the agreement, can get on with their life.

It will not be easy. As you can appreciate, your lender may be willing to provide relief but will understandably be reluctant to forego an eventual repayment of the loan that could arise from your income improving or your property increasing in value.

The MARS Long-Term Solutions May Give the Best Result for Your Lender

Your lender may achieve the best result by taking an innovative approach to the long-term solutions, for a number of reasons:

- This area of resolution remains pretty much within your lender's control. Should you move to insolvency or bankruptcy, any solution will incur costs, which will more than likely come from funds available to your lender.
- The cost of the personal insolvency practitioner and monitoring by the Insolvency Service will have to be met from your payments, thus reducing funds available to repay debt to your lender.
- In bankruptcy the legal costs and the cost of bankruptcy will generally come out of net proceeds from what may be a fire sale of assets (quick sale of assets below their market value).
- Both personal insolvency and bankruptcy have defined time periods for recoverability of debt by your lender – between three and seven years, depending on which you choose.
- A long-term deal (outside the insolvency or bankruptcy process), if structured properly, can seek to take advantage of your lifelong earnings.

There are sound reasons why, in many cases, your lender will want to do a deal that prevents you looking to the insolvency legislation for a solution to your problem. You need to appreciate this and prepare your case well.

When will I have to negotiate?

At some point in the process you will have to negotiate a deal, which you will be expected to live with for a period of time.

This may happen when you first approach the lender; for example, if you needed some latitude for six to twelve months and you expected this to be sufficient. The problem you have encountered may be temporary and solvable within months.

Alternatively, you may have a financial problem that will take longer to fix. For instance, your difficulties may be due to unemployment and the prospect of finding work may be low for the foreseeable future as your industry is in decline. Either way, you need to negotiate the right terms so that you can focus on improving your financial position and have a decent lifestyle for you and your family in the meantime.

Obviously the lender will want to stay as close to the original deal as possible – and this is probably what you want too – but circumstances may dictate that some compromise will be necessary on both sides.

Before we look at the approach you can adopt to getting the right deal from your lender it is worth looking at the art of negotiation.

What Is Negotiation?

Negotiation is simply talking to others to achieve an agreement. A negotiation situation arises at any time when two or more people have different points of view as to what is to be done in a given situation.

Most negotiators look to achieve a win–win situation. This is because most negotiations are between people who will have a long-term relationship and may need to co-operate in the future. A win–win result shares the benefits between the parties and recognises that the current negotiation is one of many that may follow. Trade union–employer negotiations, for example, require two groups with competing views to work together for many years. As you will have an ongoing relationship with your lender you should be looking for a win–win solution in which you get most of what you need and your lender gets most of what they need.

Core Concepts: The Key to Success in a Negotiation

Successful negotiation rests on four concepts.

1. Best Alternative

As you and your lender discuss the solution to your financial difficulties you will both be considering what your options are if you fail to reach agreement. This needs to be considered carefully. Remember, there are many options and each needs to be considered so that you know that the deal you agree to is an acceptable one, even if it is not your first choice.

2. Areas of Possible Agreement

Your lender will look for a solution and to achieve this they will explore a range of areas where there is common ground, which negotiators often refer to as the 'zone of possible agreement'. Every negotiation has areas of overlap where agreement is possible. The secret is to find them: they are not always obvious, and patience and skill is required to uncover them.

Your lender will want the loan repaid, but they will also want a loan that is being serviced within agreed terms and without arrears. If you can service a lesser amount, this provides the overlap to one of the Level 2 long-term solutions we discussed earlier.

3. Trading Value

This is about trading or giving in on areas that are of less value to you, but which are of exceptional value to the other side. For instance, you may be more concerned about having an acceptable lifestyle for your family while you seek to rebuild your financial position. Your lender, being more concerned with recovering their loans, may be prepared to accommodate this if you can accept deferred debt with a long-term repayment structure rather than opting for insolvency.

It is also important not to agree too easily. You may have heard the expression, 'Nothing is agreed until everything is agreed.' A good negotiator waits until they have all the points of negotiation tentatively agreed before agreeing to all points. In the case of Peter and Joan above, before they agree to the warehoused loan, they should seek clarification and agreement on the other issues, such as whether the warehoused loan will attract interest.

4. Reservation Price

Also called your 'walk-away' position, this is your least favourable point and a deal you would see no value in agreeing to. Both you and your lender will have a walk-away position, and it is important to remember this. If this point is reached it could spell the end of the negotiation with a result neither side is prepared for. Also keep in mind that under the Code of Conduct on Mortgage Arrears your lender has to work with you on a solution but is not bound to offer you one. They may decide that sale is the only solution. This is why making an assessment of all options, including bankruptcy, is important – even if you do not want to go there.

A Simple Example of Negotiation

To explain these concepts, let us look at a simple example used by trainers in negotiation skills:

> **Case Study: Negotiation**
>
> Two friends, Pat and Orla, who are next-door neighbours, have just come back from a workout at the gym.
>
> Both want an orange, but there is only one orange available. They are negotiating how to divide the orange between them. Both would like as much of the orange as they can get. The preferred position of each is to get the whole orange, as this would maximise the result for them.

They know absolutely nothing about the skills of negotiation and only argue. Each believes they have a right to the whole orange and conceals their purpose rather than explore each other's position. In the end, out of frustration, they agree to divide the orange in half.

Pat, who cooks, returns to his apartment to use his half of the orange to bake a cake. He scoops out the centre of the orange and discards it to use the orange rind in the cake.

Orla, an athlete, needs the orange to squeeze some juice. She discards the skin and uses the centre to make orange juice.

This is a simple example, but it highlights the elements of negotiation and the need to work to a formula to get the best results.

Pat and Orla did not take time to find out what the other needed and each focused purely on what they wanted. They failed to see the opportunity to trade something that had less value to them for something that was of exceptional value to the other.

Pat could have had all of what he needed, the orange skin, if he had taken the time to explore options and had been more open about his needs. The same is true of Orla.

Avoid Common Negotiation Mistakes

We will shortly apply these and some other principles to your case, but before we discuss what makes for successful negotiation let us have a look at the key mistakes.

Failure to Prepare Properly

It is an old cliché, but very true: 'Failing to plan is planning to fail.' If I stress anything in this book it is:

- You must know your figures.
- They must be accurate.
- You must assess your long-term prospects.

- You must have an idea of the solution to your problem.
- You must have your facts and be prepared to present your case.

For you the negotiations may be a traumatic experience that is new and unfamiliar, but for your lender it will be routine. This not to say that your lender will not treat you as an individual, it is just that with so many problems on their books they will have a well-rehearsed routine that has been used many times. Good preparation will allow the figures to speak for you.

Failure to Apply the Win–Win Approach

Think back to the example of the orange. Your lender will want a deal, but they will also have a walk-away position. Also, your lender may be willing to provide short-term solutions, but if you need a long-term one or you feel you need debt forgiveness you will have to get this on the agenda.

Failure to Remain Calm

Intimidating behaviour or being aggressive is a real turn-off and will get you absolutely nowhere. Losing your temper and blaming your lender for your problem will end the negotiation, as will any threat of legal action. If you are aggressive or make threats, this results in a bad atmosphere and deflects from the purpose of reaching an agreement. If it continues, at some point your lender may suggest dealing through solicitors, which will cost you money.

Failure to Listen

Listen to your lender's argument. More important, listen for areas of common ground or areas where your lender may be happy to give in.

It is important to influence rather than argue with your lender. As we will see later, there are many objectives that are important to your lender. You are better off showing that you can satisfy these than becoming aggressive, losing your temper and simply expecting that being in financial difficulties is enough to get you what you want.

We now know what to avoid, what can kill a negotiation and result in you standing in the car park wondering what went wrong. Remember, the longer you keep positive interactions going with your lender the better chance you have of getting an acceptable result. At the very least, you will discover your lender's final position – or what they say is their final position.

If this position is unacceptable you will have other options, including appointing an intermediary to work on your behalf, seeking a PIA, or perhaps bankruptcy. There are a number of avenues available, but rather than moving to these solutions too quickly and incurring expense, it is best to interact with your lender first to establish their best offer.

How to Go About a Negotiation

Below are a number of things to consider when you start your negotiation.

Choose the Right Time

While you may want to relieve the pressure of your financial difficulties as quickly as possible, it is best to do an assessment of your position first. This may mean having an initial meeting to allow your lender to outline their processes, and deferring any decisions until you have completed your own assessment. It is also possible that when you contact your lender initially they will write to you and ask you to complete the standard financial statement and bring it to your meeting.

Anticipate Counter-Arguments

You should expect your lender to have counter-arguments, such as reminding you that you signed a loan agreement, the need for a minimum level of contribution or an expectation that you will consider selling your home. This is normal and it is best to expect this rather than get rattled by it and allow it to upset the negotiations.

Be Specific About Your Needs and Wants

It may not be difficult to receive some initial support for, say, six months. However, at some point you will have to address specific solutions for the long term if your problem is that severe. An accurate assessment of your financial position both now and into the future will make this clear.

Be Tactful and Listen Carefully

The lender may not want to hear what you are about to tell them – lenders do not like bad news. So bear with the situation and remain tactful. Be prepared to compromise, but remember, the solution should be within your zone of possible agreement.

Show Willingness to Accept a Solution

Show a commitment to stick to any deal you agree. Remember, it is important to get a solution you can live up to. This will be particularly important if the negotiation is taking place in the context of a PIA, as if you break the deal you may lose the benefit you have achieved.

Now that you have a feel for the negotiation process we will look at how you can apply it to your particular situation.

The Mortgage Arrears Resolution Strategy (MARS), which is designed to deal with arrears problems in need of a long-term solution, was introduced by lenders at the request of the Central Bank of Ireland. The word 'Strategy' is interesting. When businesses look at strategy they carry out an assessment of their relative position in relation to that of their competitors. This is called a SWOT analysis:

- **S**trengths – the business's competitive strengths
- **W**eaknesses – the business's weaknesses
- **O**pportunities – the opportunities that exist for the business in the market
- **T**hreats – market threats to the business

To help you prepare for your negotiation, consider your lender's resolution strategy and what their SWOT analysis might look like, as in the following example:

Lender's SWOT Analysis

Strengths	Weaknesses
• As it is personal debt, you are liable for the full balance. • They hold security for their lending. • They can petition for your bankruptcy. • They can defer or warehouse a portion of the loan. • They can provide either interest forgiveness or debt forgiveness.	• The Code of Conduct on Mortgage Arrears restricts your lender's ability to act. • Many buy-to-let mortgages in arrears are in significant negative equity. • The property market is in a slump, which makes selling a property difficult.

(*Continued*)

Lender's SWOT Analysis (*Continued*)

Opportunities	Threats
• Long-term solutions provide an opportunity to structure a deal that may be better than one achieved if you choose the insolvency route or bankruptcy. • A performing loan is a saleable product which can relieve the lender's balance sheet. • Regularising loans, even after write-down, will eventually improve a lender's balance sheet profile and help attract investors. • Writing off some debt now with an up-side in the future may lead to windfall recoveries later.	• You can frustrate a property sale, so your co-operation is needed. • You may choose to resolve your situation using the personal insolvency legislation. • You may consider bankruptcy as an acceptable solution to your problem. • The lender's loan documentation needs to be adequate for a successful legal result. • The legal process is costly and sometimes unpredictable. • Amendments to the bankruptcy legislation may make this route expensive and uncertain.

Looking at this SWOT analysis for your lender, you can see that there are plenty of threats and weaknesses for them. You could even consider that your lender's threats and weaknesses are your strengths and opportunities and that your negotiation position may be stronger than you first imagined.

Using the four core principles outlined above and the knowledge you have gained from this book you can now put together your strategy for achieving what you want. This will involve:

- Acknowledging the problem
- Making an honest and accurate assessment of your financial position
- Assessing your future prospects and ability to pay your debts

- Assessing your eligibility for each of the mortgage arrears resolution processes:
  - MARP – short-term assistance
  - MARS – longer-term, lender-driven solutions
  - Personal insolvency – with a personal insolvency practitioner
  - Bankruptcy – court-based legal solution
- Assessing the relative strength of your position using the four core principles

How Strong Is Your Case?

Best Alternative

The SWOT analysis above indicates that the key strong points your lender has are: they may have security for some or all of the debt; and you are personally liable for any shortfall.

They will also be well aware of their responsibilities under the mortgage process and also the poor market conditions for selling buy-to-let properties. These factors may lead them to rely on their other strengths rather than adopt an aggressive approach. Also, a tougher stance can be adopted with buy-to-let properties than with family homes.

This may involve them offering a favourable deal which defers the problem into the future with a hope for recovery then or, in more severe cases, allowing an element of debt forgiveness in return for property sale. For those who are willing to consider bankruptcy, the possible outcome of this action for your lender may help focus the discussion.

Your position can be strengthened if you have done your homework, especially with the help of an adviser, and if options such as insolvency or even bankruptcy are routes that are both available and ones you are willing to take. The legal process is costly for a lender and can be uncertain as documentation and advice given will be examined.

So both you and your lender will have to analyse your best alternative to find a negotiated solution.

Areas of Possible Agreement

Remember: any solution that is available using processes such as insolvency or bankruptcy is also available at the lower-level solutions such as the MARP and MARS processes. Throughout this book I have made the point that the MARP and MARS processes focus on debt deferment rather than debt forgiveness. However, this is purely a matter of emphasis rather than formal rules.

Insolvency or bankruptcy seeks to force a solution on either party, be it debt forgiveness on the part of the lender or a sale of all assets on the part of the borrower, but either of these extremes – and any solution in between – is possible by negotiation under the MARS process if a common sense approach is taken.

Case Study

Joe has a mortgage of €400,000 and is finding the monthly payments of €2,100 too much. He is happy that his pension provision and state benefits for the rest of his life will allow him to pay €1,600, which is around the cost of renting a property in his area.

He wonders if his lender would allow him to pay €1,600 per month indefinitely. This would give him a good lifestyle, keep him in his house and allow him to pass the house mortgage to his family when he dies, or alternatively to sell the property.

To achieve this the lender would have to take a 50-year view on the property as follows:

- €400,000 mortgage at 4 per cent over 25 years = €2,111 per month
- €400,000 mortgage at 4 per cent over 50 years = €1,542 per month

At the end of 25 years the loan outstanding on the 50-year loan will be €292,000.

This simple, if somewhat extreme, example shows that in some cases new lending structures may more easily achieve a resolution than legal action. The MARS process allows these areas to be explored before investing money and time in forced solutions.

Trading Value

The idea here is to anticipate what may be of interest to the other party. Your lender will be looking for maximum recovery of the loan, but they are also looking to achieve a permanent deal that is sustainable and will not need to be revisited each year. This reduces cost and also allows them to get their lending book back in order. Reducing the loan book is also a high priority, and some lenders may be willing to forgive debt to achieve this outcome.

You may need debt forgiveness to make things work for you. In the case of buy-to-let properties, agreeing to a sale with some write-down of debt may suit. An extended period to repay residual debt may also be of benefit. The importance of avoiding bankruptcy or having a good lifestyle for your family will also need to be factored into any solution.

Case Study

Aoife is a professional who needs to avoid bankruptcy to continue earning a living. Her income has fallen dramatically due to a fall-off in her sector of work.

Aoife is now refocusing her expertise on an emerging sector and sees the potential to earn a significant income in the future. She is aware of the insolvency legislation and how it may achieve debt forgiveness, but wants to avoid the austerity and possible requirement to trade down her house.

She can service interest but would like to achieve some debt forgiveness if possible. The most important factor for

---

her is having an acceptable and sustainable deal for her family so that she can focus on the future.

Rather than focus solely on debt forgiveness, Aoife is seeking to trade, using the following trade-offs:

- She wants to forge a deal outside the insolvency structure.
- She wants to remain in the house.
- She will sell non-essential assets to reduce debt, with an element of debt forgiveness.
- Rather than suffer too much austerity, she will seek to structure a plan whereby her lender will have 40 per cent of her disposable income towards her interest and capital.
- When her income increases above an agreed threshold the percentage above this level increases to 60 per cent.
- Should the lenders make her bankrupt her earning power will cease.

Using this approach, Aoife calculates that her lender will avoid legal expenses now, have a sustainable repayment plan and will, in the longer term, achieve a higher recovery on their debt.

She and her adviser support her case with calculations and comparative analysis outlining the likely recovery of her lender should Aoife have to use the personal insolvency route or the bankruptcy route.

The above example highlights that there may be things that can be traded to help you achieve an acceptable result. The provision of comparative analysis helps with a discussion around the next best alternative for both parties.

It is important that you consider carefully with your adviser what you want to achieve and how you can convince your lender that it is in their interest to agree. You may also have to adjust your demands and be prepared to compromise on some issues – but that is negotiation for you.

Reservation Price

You need to establish what this is, but it is not something you should rush, particularly in relation to your family home. The MARP code provides plenty of time to explore options. As already stated, the key is to assess your finances, and it is best to get professional advice in this regard.

After you have assessed your possible outcomes under the various processes, have an adviser negotiate for you if your position is severe. When you are agreeing your budgets with your lender under the mortgage arrears process it may make sense to budget for the cost of an adviser – with agreement from your lender. This may mean less for them in the short term but may facilitate a meaningful discussion and a less costly solution in the long run.

Calculate Your Lifetime Earnings

One of the objectives of this book is to encourage you to look at your financial future as a whole and not just the particular difficulty you have at present. Doing this may provide more clarity on how to solve the problem in the context of having a reasonable living standard and an acceptable retirement.

In order to do this it may be useful to calculate your lifetime earnings. Most of us can predict with some accuracy what this figure will be as we are likely to be in the same job sector for the rest of our lives. You can also make assumptions about your possible salary growth if you wish, but be conservative.

Case Study

Patrick, who is 40, is married with two children aged 9 and 10. His wife, Kate, works in the home.

Patrick has a solid job and expects to remain in it until retirement at age 65. He receives a current net after-tax salary

---

of €54,000 and calculates that his net pension, including state benefits, will average €47,000 from age 65. He will receive a tax-free pension lump sum of €120,000 at 65. He is also expecting an inheritance of €100,000.

So what are the lifetime earnings available to satisfy the family's financial demands?

- €54,000 at an average growth rate of 3 per cent over 25 years will accumulate to €1,970,000
- Pension lump sum of €120,000
- Pension after age 65 for 20 years (assume no increase) amounts to €940,000
- Inheritance of €100,000
- **Total lifetime income is €3,130,000**

This excludes the value on any property assets which can be sold in the future.

This is a simplified example and while the figure looks large this is an estimated *total* fund available to Patrick over the 45-year period. From this Patrick has to accommodate:

- An anticipated acceptable lifestyle for him and his family from now until retirement
- Education and other expenses for his children
- A reasonable lifestyle in retirement
- The repayment of all debt

In structuring a deal with his lenders, Patrick would do well to consider the long term and, depending on his debt position and serviceability, seek to achieve a deal that satisfies his overall goals. This may involve a sale of assets, the deferment of debt, interest forgiveness or debt forgiveness, and commitments around partial lump-sum payments.

SUMMARY

No matter what resolution process you use it will involve negotiation. At personal insolvency level you will have to use a personal insolvency practitioner. However, to have the best chance of avoiding this option it may be better to engage an adviser earlier.

The negotiation will revolve around the core principles of best alternative, areas of possible agreement, trading value and reservation price, so focus on how you can use these to structure your deal. Also, remember the tips and the common mistakes that can be made, and remember that the process can take some time – do not lose patience.

Key Points in this Chapter

1. All the mortgage arrears resolution processes will involve negotiation.
2. Focus on the core principles outlined in the chapter and seek to adapt them to your situation.
3. Best results may be achieved using a professional and experienced adviser.
4. Avoid common mistakes (like losing your temper) and be patient.
5. Do a SWOT analysis to see what you can offer your lender.
6. Seek out areas of common ground that can be part of a solution.
7. Be prepared to compromise and look for trade-offs.
8. Do your homework on what options are available to you, even though you may not want to use them.
9. Work out what is acceptable to you and what is not.
10. Remember that negotiation is a process. The longer you stay engaged, the longer you stay in your home and the more time you have to get back on your feet.

Part II

The Mortgage Arrears Resolution Process (MARP): Your Lender's Short-Term Solutions to Mortgage Arrears

This part of the book looks at the Mortgage Arrears Resolution Process (MARP) in more detail and shows you how to approach each of the steps in this five-step process.

I will stress the importance of full engagement with your lender, including the provision of full and accurate financial information. I will also work with you to achieve an accurate assessment of your financial position both now and into the future and show you that if this is done properly the solution to your financial difficulties should be clear.

Finally, I outline your options should you and your lender fail to agree on a common approach.

5

An Introduction to MARP

The man who can drive himself further once the effort gets painful is the man who will win.
Sir Roger Bannister, British athlete and the first man to run the four-minute mile

In Part I of this book we split the solutions available into four levels. Over the next three chapters we will examine the Level 1 remedy being proposed to deal with the personal debt crisis in this country. At this level the aim is to relieve the cash flow burden on the borrower and allow them to stay in their family home.

As this point there is no talk of debt forgiveness on your debt, so the arrangements proposed by your lender will more than likely ease your monthly payments and allow you to remain in your home, but leave you with the same level of debt. Depending on your circumstances that may be acceptable to you, but it is important that you explore all options and ensure that any deal you do is something you can live with.

The five-step approach (outlined in Chapter 3) that lenders use to deal with loans in difficulty has been formalised by the Central Bank under the Code of Conduct on Mortgage Arrears. This provides a formal structure and guidance to lenders on how they should work with mortgage holders in arrears.

The five-step process is called the Mortgage Arrears Resolution Process (MARP). The five stages of the process are:

- Step 1: Communication with borrowers
- Step 2: Financial information
- Step 3: Assessment
- Step 4: Resolution
- Step 5: Appeals

Definitions and Meanings

We will describe each step of the MARP in more detail later and highlight the importance of each step, as this process and its outcome requires your careful consideration. To use MARP successfully it is useful to remember a number of key elements in the process, outlined below.

The Objective Is to Keep You in Your Home if Possible

The objective of MARP, and also the aim of the insolvency legislation, which will be discussed in Part IV, is to find a solution that does not involve the sale of the family home. You can gain a lot of comfort from this.

Engagement

In order to gain the protections afforded by the Code of Conduct on Mortgage Arrears you must engage fully in the process. This means providing full disclosure of your financial position and adhering to any initial loan modification agreement with your lender.

It Is a Process

It is important to appreciate that MARP is a process. Like all processes, it moves from one stage to the next and should end in a result. That result will not necessarily be your desired outcome, so it is important to take each stage slowly and ensure that you are happy with how the process is developing.

In reaching the final outcome, particularly in very difficult cases, further remedies – such as the protections afforded by the insolvency or bankruptcy legislation – will be on the mind of your lender and may prompt an agreed solution.

There Is No Eleventh Hour

MARP lacks an eleventh hour. By this I mean that even though there are deadlines, the process may go on for some time. Even if an agreed initial solution breaks down, the process can usually be started again if there is genuine need. Bearing this in mind, the fact is that once you engage with the process and co-operate with your lender, staying in your home for quite a while is very feasible, and this can provide enough time for you to get back on your feet.

MARP has the potential to go on for many years without achieving an outcome other than the borrower staying in their home with their existing level of debt. It is unlikely that your lender will be rushing the process or aggressively looking for you to leave your home.

There is also no debt forgiveness inherent in MARP, and the lender will not automatically offer debt forgiveness. This is partly because MARP is designed to allow people to stay in their homes, but it is also because it lacks an eleventh-hour deadline where a permanent solution must be reached. Of course there are timelines and ramifications for those who do not engage, but in general it is hard to see how anybody who engages genuinely with their lender can lose their house in the medium term.

In most negotiations, such as labour talks, there is a point at which either both sides agree to a solution or something final happens, such as a company closure or an employee strike. The eleventh-hour position forces a solution to a situation as each party weighs up the consequences of not reaching agreement. Not to agree or find common ground will have consequences for each side, so they must consider carefully whether finding a compromise is best.

Is this good or bad?

The lack of an effective eleventh hour in MARP can be seen by either party as a good or bad thing. From the bank's point of view it can be good if they are at least being paid their interest, or even some capital, and they defer the ultimate repayment of the loan until things improve. On the other hand, if the borrower has no ability to pay and does not look as if they ever will, the process can slow their ability to take appropriate action.

For a borrower who has a short-term problem and is not excessively in debt the process can be a help in ensuring that the bank does not act prematurely in forcing a house sale. If, however, the problems are more severe and the borrower needs debt forgiveness, the process may frustrate this somewhat as debt forgiveness is not automatically on the agenda, and the lender may prefer to manage the situation differently. To achieve debt forgiveness at these lower levels of discussion the borrower needs to drive the agenda and be prepared to consider insolvency or even bankruptcy to get what they want.

The Code of Conduct on Mortgage Arrears

Purpose of the Code

The purpose of the Code of Conduct on Mortgage Arrears (issued under Section 117 of the Central Bank Act 1989) is explained in its introduction:

> This Code sets out how mortgage lenders (referred to in this document as 'lenders') must treat **borrowers** in or facing mortgage **arrears**, with due regard to the fact that

each case of mortgage arrears is unique and needs to be considered on its own merits. This Code sets out the framework that lenders must use when dealing with borrowers in mortgage arrears or in **pre-arrears**. All such cases must be handled sympathetically and positively by the lender, with the objective at all times of assisting the **borrower** to meet his/her mortgage obligations.

The words in bold have defined meanings within the Code:

- **Arrears** – Arrears arise on a mortgage loan account where a borrower has not made a full mortgage repayment, or only makes a partial mortgage repayment, as per the original mortgage contract, by the scheduled due date.
- **Borrower** – This includes all parties named on the mortgage loan account.
- **Pre-arrears** – A pre-arrears case arises where the borrower contacts the lender to inform them that he/she is in danger of going into financial difficulties and/or is concerned about going into mortgage arrears.

From the above extract it can be seen that the Central Bank has put in place a structure that seeks to create a level playing field between you and your lender. This provides the space to find a resolution to your problem while allowing you to remain in your home. It is important, as you will see in this part of the book, that you know and follow the Code, because it is your key protection in the case of financial difficulties with your house.

The Code Only Applies to Your Primary Residence

One point to note, particularly if you have more than one property, is that the Code applies to your primary residence. As defined in Chapter 2 of the Code, 'primary residence' means a property that is:

(i) the residential property which the borrower occupies as his/her primary residence in this State, or

(ii) a residential property in this State which is the only residential property owned by the borrower.

What this means is that if you have more than one property, only the one used as your primary residence is covered by the Code. The other properties may fall into the category of investment properties, or what are commonly called buy-to-let properties, and they are not covered by the Code. (We will look at these in Part III.)

The good news for people who have rented out their property and who are in difficulty is that if this is your only property it is also treated under the Code as your primary residence, even if you are not living in it. This protection is conditional on the property being within the state. Sole properties abroad are not covered.

You may feel that the protection of the Code should extend to all properties, but its purpose is strictly focused on protecting people in difficulties with their family home. The idea is to set out how mortgage lenders – your lender – treat borrowers who face mortgage arrears. It recognises that it is in the interest of both you and your lender to address financial difficulties quickly, but seeks to ensure a balance in the relationship so that you are treated reasonably and sympathetically.

Engagement and Co-Operation Are Vital

The fact that there is an emphasis on keeping you in your home does not mean that the Code is totally on your side. It places an onus on you, as the borrower, to provide certain information and engage with the process in order to continue to have its protection.

This is important. The Code offers real protection and significant time to sort out your difficulties, but a condition of this support is that you engage with your lender. If you are considered to be not co-operating you may lose the protection of the Code, so ignoring your problem is not a good strategy.

What is meant by 'not co-operating'? The definition provided in Chapter 2 of the Code is:

A borrower can be considered as not co-operating with the lender when any of the following apply to their particular case:

(a) the borrower fails to make a full and honest disclosure of information to the lender, that would have a significant impact on their financial situation;
(b) the borrower fails to provide information sought by the lender relevant to the borrower's financial situation; or
(c) a three-month period elapses during which the borrower:
  (i) has failed to meet his/her mortgage repayments in full as per the mortgage contract or has failed to meet in full repayments as specified in the terms of an alternative repayment arrangement; and
  (ii) has not made contact with, or responded to, any communications from the lender or a third party acting on the lender's behalf.

The new consultation process being undertaken by the Central Bank in relation to MARP will consider an appropriate notice period and timeframe for your lender to seek repossession in the case of non-co-operation. This emphasises how essential it is to engage with your lender once a problem arises and also to stay engaged with the process.

Full Disclosure and Adherence to Agreements

The Code's definition of non-co-operation quoted above also touches on two other points that are central to the process (we shall look at these in detail later in the book).

The first is that the process requires full and honest disclosure of your financial position and for you to respond to your lender's requests for information. This need not be a daunting exercise, and the better you prepare for this the better your chance of getting the deal you want.

The second item that is touched on is a breach of your mortgage terms. While the reason you are in the mortgage arrears process may be because you have breached the terms of your mortgage, the definition also includes a situation where the borrower 'has failed to meet in full repayments as specified in the terms of an alternative repayment arrangement'. This refers to any latitude, such as an interest-only period, your lender has provided. You will be required to sign your acceptance to this, so you must ensure that you only agree to what you can live up to. However, if the breach is due to genuine need and you inform your lender of this, they are likely to reopen discussions on a solution. The key point is not to ignore the problem.

What if I am not in arrears but may be soon – can I get the protection of the Code?

The Code also provides protection to people who are in what is called pre-arrears. I outlined the definition of pre-arrears earlier in this chapter, but let us look at it again. Chapter 2 of the Code states:

> A pre-arrears case arises where the borrower contacts the lender to inform them that he/she is in danger of going into financial difficulties and/or is concerned about going into mortgage arrears.

What this is saying is that you do not have to be actually in arrears to start the process and gain the protection of the Code. If you feel it is likely that you will go into arrears, you can contact your lender straight away and start the process of dealing with the situation. It may be preferable to achieve some initial short-term latitude while you assess the gravity of the situation.

A pre-arrears situation may occur as a result of an event such as loss of employment or illness; while you may not be in arrears at present, you are worried that this may happen. If you inform your lender of your position you will come within the process outlined in the Code.

It is advisable to inform your lender early if you suspect arrears will arise, rather than waiting until you are actually in arrears. This is to your advantage as it allows time to look at options before the arrears arise. One option that may be considered is moving to an interest-only period, and this may be easier to achieve before a payment is missed.

The Borrower Is Not Just You

The definition of 'borrower' may seem obvious enough, but the definition in the Code can include more than the obvious borrower: it 'includes *all* parties named on the mortgage loan account'. This might include parents who have provided support to a son or daughter to help them obtain the loan and have in the process joined themselves into the mortgage.

It also includes those who have separated or are in the course of doing so. If the party to the mortgage who is making the repayments can no longer do so and requires the assistance of the Code, the other party is automatically brought into the process, with the requirement to provide the same level of information regarding their financial position. ·

Many of the issues raised will be dealt with throughout the book, and the implications for individuals will be discussed.

SUMMARY

At the core of the Code of Conduct on Mortgage Arrears is the Mortgage Arrears Resolution Process (MARP). This is the structure of the negotiation that will take place between borrowers and their lenders as set out by the Central Bank. Lenders are required under the Code to have such a process in place. The process seeks to achieve the following for you in relation to your lender:

- You will be treated fairly by the lender.
- The process is the same for all borrowers and is transparent.
- The lender must explain clearly your options for rescheduling your loan.
- The lender is prohibited from harassing you and from imposing penalty charges.
- The lender must stick to any new agreement, provided that you do too.

The purpose of MARP is not to provide an advantage to either party, and you would be naive to believe that it gives you the upper hand; however, it does level the playing field to allow for a possible resolution.

It is vital that you engage in the process should your mortgage go into arrears or is likely to do so, as the Code is your protection and may keep you in your home long enough to resolve your difficulties and get back on your feet. The Code does not directly apply to investment or buy-to-let mortgages in arrears; however, your lender's approach to these is likely to be quite similar, at least initially. (We will discuss these mortgages in Chapter 11.)

It is important to co-operate with your lender and to provide all information requested. This is standard for all lenders and, as we shall see in Chapter 7, if you do this properly the solution you need will become obvious.

Remember to include all parties to the loan in the discussion as they may not have the same options available as you do and will need to do their own deal with your lender.

The MARP process provides short-term relief to allow you get back on your feet. Should you need a more permanent solution it may be best to talk to an adviser.

Key Points in this Chapter

1. The Code of Conduct on Mortgage Arrears was set up for your benefit and provides a framework to resolve your financial difficulties with your lender.
2. The Code only applies to your primary residence. Investment properties are excluded unless the property is your only property in the state.
3. Your lender will have to follow the process outlined in the Code in their dealings with you.
4. To achieve the protection of the Code you will have to engage with your lender and remain co-operative in the provision of accurate information.
5. Even if you are currently within the terms of your mortgage but are experiencing financial difficulties, you can contact your lender and seek the protection of the Code. This is referred to as a pre-arrears situation.
6. The process has five successive steps, which can take some time to complete:
    i. Step 1: Communication with borrowers
    ii. Step 2: Financial information
    iii. Step 3: Assessment
    iv. Step 4: Resolution
    v. Step 5: Appeals
7. It is best to understand how the process works and stick with it while you look to get back on your feet.
8. There is no automatic debt forgiveness in the process, so you will have to put debt forgiveness on the agenda if that is what you require.

---

9. The borrower is not just you, but all parties to the mortgage. If there is a guarantor, get them involved early on.
10. If debt forgiveness is what you need, be prepared to consider moving to insolvency and seeking professional advice on this rather than hoping for it under MARP.

6

Communicating with Your Lender

He who has learned to disagree without being disagreeable
has discovered the most valuable secret of a diplomat.
Robert Estabrook, US publisher, editor and newspaper owner

Starting the Journey

We have seen that the Code of Conduct on Mortgage
Arrears seeks to put in place a structure to achieve agreement on your financial difficulties. This ensures that you as
the borrower are dealt with in an open and transparent way.
It also ensures that all options to resolve the arrears or potential arrears are looked at.

As already explained, 'the borrower' refers to all parties
to the mortgage loan account, so everybody named on the
mortgage will be asked to engage in the process. The reason
for this is that if the lender agrees to some alteration in the
terms of your mortgage, even for a short period, they will
require all parties to agree. Not getting this agreement before
going ahead with the alteration could cause the lender legal
problems later. Accordingly, everybody will have to agree to
any modification to the loan and will be required to provide
details of their financial position.

You will also have responsibilities, which will be explained
later, and these must be observed to achieve the protection
of the Code. The five-step process will allow you and your
lender to set out your respective stalls to ensure that all

information is on the table and all avenues for resolution can be explored. As we have seen, the five-step process is:

- Step 1: Communication with borrowers
- Step 2: Financial information
- Step 3: Assessment
- Step 4: Resolution
- Step 5: Appeals

In this chapter we will look at Steps 1 and 2.

Step 1: Communication – Getting the Right Start

Step 1 – communication – relates to communication between the lender and you. It is designed to encourage open engagement between you. This communication may start with you advising your lender either orally or in writing that you have a problem and need to meet with them to discuss options. If you do not contact your lender at the first sign of trouble, they will call you when the mortgage goes into arrears: in fact, the Code requires them to do so:

> As soon as a borrower goes into arrears, a lender must communicate promptly and clearly with the borrower to establish in the first instance why the repayment schedule as per the mortgage contract, has not been adhered to.
>
> *Code of Conduct on Mortgage Arrears 2010*
> *(Chapter 3, Clause 7)*

So either way, this first step is intended to start the conversation on a possible resolution of your mortgage arrears and is worth engaging in early.

When will my lender contact me?

If you miss a mortgage payment your lender will obviously want to know why. It may be just an oversight, such as a late transfer or delayed salary payment, or it could be a one-off shortfall. The Code requires your lender to contact you promptly when a mortgage payment is missed. You can expect to receive a letter or phone call from your lender within seven to ten days of any arrears if the account is not brought up to date straight away.

The main concern your lender will have is whether the missed payment is due to changed financial circumstances and, more specifically, whether you will have difficulty in meeting your future repayments in whole or in part.

Your lender is required to actively encourage you to engage with them should you be in financial difficulties. It is important that you respond to this offer – not doing so may result in you losing the protection the Code affords. Also, your lender will not be able to impose charges on your arrears if you are covered by the Code and are co-operating in a reasonable manner.

Do not be intimidated, angry with your lender or ignore the problem. It is better to embrace the process and place the problem with the lender for both of you to resolve. This gives you the protection of the Code – and putting the problem on the table will help relieve stress.

When should I contact my lender?

If a life event happens that will result in your being unable to pay mortgage repayments, or if you have a concern that you may not be able to make a payment, the first step is to advise your lender. The key thing to understand now is that making the lender aware of your situation places you within the Code and provides a framework to resolve your difficulties.

Another benefit of early contact and engagement with your lender is that the lender is only allowed to contact you three times in any one month. This is designed to prevent multiple annoying calls from your lender. The Code states:

Each calendar month, a lender, and/or any third party acting on its behalf, may not initiate more than three unsolicited communications, by whatever means, to a borrower in respect of his/her mortgage arrears or pre-arrears situation.

The unsolicited communications do not include any communications to the borrower regarding his/her arrears or pre-arrears situation, which are required by this Code or other regulatory requirements.

Code of Conduct on Mortgage Arrears 2010
(Chapter 3, Clause 21)

Unless you have asked your lender to contact you or given them permission to contact you in relation to your arrears situation, they are only allowed to contact you three times each calendar month in relation to your mortgage. This includes contact by phone, by email, by text message or by letter. The new consultation process being undertaken by the Central Bank in relation to MARP will consider the effectiveness of the current unsolicited contact terms and what constitutes not co-operating with your lender. Proposed changes are unlikely to impact those who fully engage in the process.

The above extract also states that the contact excludes communication allowed under the Code or other regulatory requirements. This refers mainly to letters sent to you reminding you of the arrears, outstanding amounts and the ramifications of such arrears. The three permitted unsolicited contacts are in addition to this to allow the lender to engage with you to resolve the problem without them harassing you on a daily basis.

In summary, by making contact with your lender you bring yourself within the mortgage Code, you enter a formal process that can help you resolve your difficulties and you ensure that communication between you and your lender is not excessive.

When do you automatically enter into the process?

Despite the protection afforded by the Code, some people may be tempted to ignore the situation for some time, but this will not be possible. The Code places responsibilities on your lender in this regard. It states:

A lender must ensure that the MARP framework is applied to the following cases:

(a) a mortgage account where arrears have arisen on the account and remain outstanding, 31 days from the date the arrears arose;

(b) a pre-arrears case;

(c) where an alternative repayment arrangement put in place breaks down; and

(d) where the term of an alternative repayment arrange-ment put in place expires.

Code of Conduct on Mortgage Arrears 2010
(Chapter 3, Clause 17)

If your mortgage account goes into arrears and the arrears remain outstanding for 31 days your lender must, under the Code, write to you and inform you of the status of your account.

The letter must, among other things:

1. State the date the mortgage fell into arrears, the number and total amount of full or partial payments missed and the amount of the arrears in euros.

2. Highlight the importance of you co-operating with the lender during the MARP process and notify you that, if co-operation stops, the protections of the MARP no longer apply and the lender may start legal proceed-ings for repossession.

3. Confirm that it is treating your case as a MARP case.

4. Include a statement that fees, charges and penalty interest in relation to the arrears will apply (and what they are) where you do not co-operate with the lender.
5. Include the information booklet on the MARP process.
Paraphrased from the Code of Conduct on Mortgage Arrears 2010
(Chapter 3, Clause 22)

What should I do when I receive the letter?

First of all, do not panic. Second, take action. Not responding to the letter will strengthen the lender's position if they wish to take action, since they will have done what is required under the Code to engage with you. Remember, engagement and co-operation with your lender gives you the best chance of being able to remain in your home until you decide on the best way forward. Let me remind you what not co-operating means:

A borrower can be considered as not co-operating with the lender when any of the following apply to their particular case:

(a) the borrower fails to make a full and honest disclosure of information to the lender, that would have a signifi-cant impact on their financial situation;
(b) the borrower fails to provide information sought by the lender relevant to the borrower's financial situa-tion; or
(c) a three-month period elapses during which the borrower:
   (i) has failed to meet his/her mortgage repayments in full as per the mortgage contract or has failed to meet in full repayments as specified in the terms of an alternative repayment arrangement; and

(ii) has not made contact with, or responded to, any communications from the lender or a third party acting on the lender's behalf.

> *Code of Conduct on Mortgage Arrears 2010*
> *(Definitions)*

Paragraph c (ii) in the above definition of non-co-operation is quite clear when it states that not responding to contact from your lender can be construed as not co-operating, and this may bring you outside the protection of the Code.

When can the lender take legal action?

Once you are co-operating the Code is quite specific that the lender cannot take action for twelve months. The twelve months excludes a number of additional time periods (which we will go into later in the book). It could take as long as two years for a lender to achieve a repossession of your house – even if that is their objective (which it is not). The Code states:

> The lender must not apply to the courts to commence legal action for repossession of the borrower's primary residence, until every reasonable effort has been made to agree an alternative arrangement with the borrower or his/her nominated representative.
>
> Where a borrower co-operates with the lender, the lender must wait at least twelve months from the date the borrower is classified as a MARP case (i.e. day 31), before applying to the courts to commence legal action for repossession of a borrower's primary residence.

> *Code of Conduct on Mortgage Arrears 2010*
> *(Chapter 3, Clauses 46 and 47)*

In Chapter 4 on negotiation we looked at the specific strategies you can adopt to deal with your lender; however, it is worth repeating that the repossession process is long and arduous for the lender. If you receive letters with repossession mentioned at an early stage in the process there is no immediate need to be anxious once you start to engage with the lender. The new consultation process on MARP will consider the appropriate notice period prior to repossession proceedings commencing in cases where an offer of support is not provided by your lender.

Step 2: Financial Information

Whether you contacted your lender or they contacted you makes no difference to this part of the process. You are both aware that you are finding it difficult to keep to your mortgage terms. The earlier both parties realise that there is a problem, the more time there is to explore options before an arrears situation arises.

Accurate Financial Information Is Key

The purpose of this information-gathering step is to establish just how much difficulty you are in. The information you provide will form the basis of the options discussed and the solution arrived at. This is perhaps the most important part of the process for you and it needs your full and active attention. The key is to ensure that you accurately assess your financial position and future prospects.

The Code makes certain requirements of you, and after the need to engage with the process the next step is full disclosure of your financial position. I will show you how to do this later, but failure to do this can be a deal-breaker. You must accurately disclose the current state of your financial position and expect your lender to look at it closely and carry out appropriate checks.

The Code places the following three specific responsibilities on your lender:

In relation to all MARP cases, a lender must:

(a) ensure the borrower understands the MARP process;
(b) provide the borrower with a standard financial statement;
(c) inform the borrower that he/she may wish to seek independent advice to assist with completing the standard financial statement, e.g., from MABS or an appropriate alternative.

> Code of Conduct on Mortgage Arrears 2010
> (Chapter 3, Clause 27)

So a lender must use a standard financial statement to obtain financial information from a borrower in arrears or in pre-arrears. The lender may also require the borrower to provide supporting documentation to confirm the information provided in the standard financial statement. These forms are standard to all lenders, as agreed with the Central Bank, so do not take the request personally. The Code states:

> The lender may require the borrower to provide supporting documentation to corroborate the information provided in the standard financial statement.

> Code of Conduct on Mortgage Arrears 2010
> (Chapter 3, Clause 29)

The Standard Financial Statement Is Your Friend

The same standard financial statement is used by all lenders and has been agreed with the Central Bank of Ireland. It is a detailed document designed to establish your income and expenditure and your assets and liabilities. As stated above, it must be completed accurately.

You may initially see this document as a threat. However, for those in genuine difficulty it is an opportunity. The opportunity is to clinically assess your situation and put it down on paper. If the statement is completed properly, the solution to your problem will become evident. The mistake people can make here is not giving the document due attention and not recording all expenses.

The deal you do with your lender will be based on these figures, so if you leave anything out you may struggle to keep to any new deal. Also your lender will scrutinise the statement and seek to pare back some items. Chapter 7 is devoted to getting this exercise right.

When you approach your lender to advise them that you may have difficulty making the repayments, they will want to know the extent of the difficulty. Is it that you cannot make *any* repayment, or is *some* level of repayment achievable? Your ability to make repayments on your mortgage can range from inability to pay any amount of the monthly payment to payment of the full amount. Between these extremes, perhaps you can only pay part of the monthly interest, or full interest with a contribution to capital. There are seven options specifically outlined in the Code, and your lender must go over these with you.

Getting Your Desired Result Is Not Automatic

You do not get to decide which options you want, so calling your lender and requesting a new payment deal will not automatically result in a positive response. Under the Code you must provide full details of your financial position on the standard financial statement. You can obtain a copy of this form from your lender's website, and you will see right away that it is very detailed in what it requires from you.

You will be requested to sign the financial statement to confirm that it is accurate and also commit to advising the lender if anything changes. This is important because, while it is not a requirement that this form is sworn, if you progress to insolvency or bankruptcy you will have to do so, and any new assets introduced later could undermine your case.

What information will I have to provide?

There are three questions that your lender will consider when they are told that you are unable to meet the terms of your mortgage:

1. What are you worth financially? This is effectively your net asset position.
2. What is your income and expenditure? This will determine your ability to service the loan.
3. What does your financial future look like? This will determine how quickly you will be able to return to full repayments.

The standard financial statement will answer questions 1 and 2, and the interview that follows will answer question 3.

The Standard Financial Statement

The main sections of the form are as follows:

Section A

This includes an outline of the basic information about your account with the lender, including the outstanding mortgage, monthly repayments and value of your primary residence. It also covers your current employment, or previous employment if you are currently unemployed, and the reason for the review or arrears.

Section B

This section seeks to establish your monthly income, whether from a salary, social welfare benefit, child benefit or family support, i.e. your total income from whatever source. This gives the lender the figure that you must work with to fund your lifestyle and pay any loan commitments.

Section C

This section looks at your household expenditure in detail. It is, perhaps, the section that needs most of your attention. Your income in Section B is probably easy to determine and may be fixed for the foreseeable future; therefore how you calculate your expenses is important in your negotiation with your lender and also your long-term decision about how to resolve your situation. Understating your expenditure could result in you signing an unsustainable deal.

Section D

This section seeks to establish the full extent of your debt from all lenders, not just your mortgage lender. This includes credit cards, store cards, hire purchase and a lot more. It may be that you are employed, but it is the extent of your debt which is causing you a problem with making mortgage payments. You may need some latitude from your mortgage lender until other short-term debt is repaid. Your mortgage lender will want to know the full extent of your debt level and your agreed repayment levels. They will also want to know whether you have spoken to these other lenders with a view to rescheduling their repayments.

Section E

This includes any property assets you may have other than your primary residence. It requires full details of the property type, ownership percentage, loan balance, valuation, monthly rental, and a lot more, including whether there are arrears on the property/ies.

Again, your mortgage lender will want to assess whether payment to other lenders is being preferred to the mortgage and whether you have sought a restructuring of other debt. Also, if you have equity in these other properties the sale of property may be on the agenda when possible solutions are being looked at.

Section F

This section seeks to establish whether you have other assets, including savings, motor vehicles, shares or other investments. If you have been made redundant your lender will want to know whether you received a redundancy payment and how this will be or has been used.

True and Correct Statement

The final thing you will have to do is sign the form and consent to a credit reference check. You will be making a declaration along the following lines:

> I declare that the information I have provided represents my/our financial situation, and commit to informing my lender if my situation changes. I consent to you conducting a credit reference check.

As your lender will carry out a credit check to confirm that your disclosure is accurate, it is important that you disclose your full financial position. Also, if undisclosed assets or cash are found later this will undermine trust between you and the lender and may stall a resolution.

Based on the information in the form, the lender will enter into discussion with you on the most appropriate payment method going forward. They will also advise you that you may wish to seek independent advice.

As the financial information will be used in assisting your case, it is important that it is accurate. This means that not only should you include all your assets and liabilities, but you also need to make an accurate assessment of your income and, more important, your expenditure or outgoings. The next chapter will help you with this.

SUMMARY

Once you realise that you have a financial difficulty it makes sense to contact your lender to share the problem and search for the solution. They will require full disclosure of financial information – without this you may lose the protection of the Code set up to deal with mortgage arrears.

The standard financial statement is the foundation of everything you will do in the process and it needs your full attention. The reason for this is that it will prove your ability, or lack of it, to repay your mortgage, and it may also be used as part of your case for insolvency should you take this route in the future. Your lender will suggest that you take independent advice or contact MABS, and this is worth considering, particularly if your problems are acute.

The information provided will be used in the resolution phase of the process, and it must be accurate. In the next chapter we shall look at assessing your financial position before moving on to look at how your lender assesses your case.

Key Points in this Chapter

1. If you are having difficulty repaying your mortgage, contact your lender before they contact you.
2. Engage fully with the process. Not only will this ease your stress, but in most cases it will also allow you to remain in your house for some time, possibly up to two years.
3. Your lender is restricted to three unsolicited contacts per month (which can help prevent stress and worry).

---

4. Your lender is obliged to inform you of the legal ramifications of not paying your mortgage, and these will be contained in any correspondence and reminder notices. However, stay focused on finding a solution within the process.
5. Provide full financial information. This will set the foundation for achieving the right outcome and will ensure no loss of credibility if anything left out comes to light later.
6. Ensure you give the standard financial statement your full attention.
7. As your income will be clear at this stage, it is important to be thorough in your assessment of all expenses. Once a new deal is struck, any items you forget to include will have to come from your limited resources.
8. Be prepared to fight your corner on the solution you need, either short-term or long-term.
9. Make a realistic assessment of your financial position, both currently and for the future. This will help you to be realistic about the solution.
10. Stay engaged with the process.
11. Seek independent advice if you are unsure of what is being proposed.

7

Assessing Your Financial Position

Money isn't the most important thing in life, but it's reasonably close to oxygen on the 'gotta have it' scale.
Zig Ziglar, US author and motivational speaker

When you fall into arrears, or are likely to do so, your lender is bound to assist you. The emphasis of MARP and the insolvency process is to keep you in your home and provide you with a reasonable standard of living.

The standard of living will be based on a negotiation between you and your lender. You will obviously want to pay as much as you can and your lender will appreciate this. However, it is up to you to ensure that the correct balance is struck. Obviously, you cannot overplay your hand and look for an expensive lifestyle while not paying your mortgage, but you need to know your figures and put a convincing case for the expenses you need to incur. Life can get very de-motivating without money, and you need to retain your energy to work yourself out of this situation.

Why is an accurate financial assessment so vital?

I have stressed that the cornerstone of MARP is an accurate assessment of your financial position. In fact, at mortgage arrears solutions Level 3 (insolvency) and Level 4 (bankruptcy), providing inaccurate financial statements can unwind any deal you achieve if it is proved at a later date that you tried to hide assets.

However, at this early stage, if you fail to give your financial assessment due consideration, it can put you at a disadvantage

When we explore budgeting below I will be encouraging you to forensically examine all your spending to ensure that *every necessary item* is included. Many people will fill out the financial statements supplied by their lender and leave out expenses that are essential to their living standard. If after doing your deal with your lender you have to make these unrecorded expenditures you may find that you are unable to keep to the deal agreed and may go into default again.

Case Study

Joan is in financial difficulties and is seeking assistance under MARP. She has completed the standard financial statement and, based on her recorded income and outgoings, has now agreed to pay interest and part capital of €700 per month. Three months into the deal Joan is financially tight and wonders why.

After reviewing her bank statements she realises that the financial statement she provided her lender did not include a number of items:

- Joan has a pedigree dog, which she now realises is costing her a fortune each year:

Kennelling fees	€200
Pet insurance	€200
Food	€500
Vet bills	€500
Total	**€1,400**

- She has a number of nieces and nephews, and she buys Christmas and birthday presents for each of them. This adds up to €500 per year.
- Joan also has a medical condition which, after state supports and tax rebates, is costing her €800 per year.

She failed to record all the above items on the financial statement she provided to her lender to support her case for assistance.

Joan is now €2,700 per year (or €225 per month) less well off than she calculated when she prepared her financial statement. She is now finding life tight, and she is in danger of going into arrears again.

The moral of the story is: *Do not expect your lender to dig every expense out of you.* If your statement makes it look as though you can pay interest and an element of capital, your lender will look for that outcome.

Your lender will also scrutinise your expenses and may look for cutbacks on some of them. Remember, this process is a negotiation, so be ready to defend those expenses that are absolutely necessary.

As I have mentioned, the key questions in your lender's mind will be:

- How much are you worth?
- How much do you currently earn?
- Is the problem short-term or long-term?

You may be tempted to leave the process to your lender on the basis that they will come up with the solution that best fits your situation. In some cases this will work well, but in others it may not be the best approach. There are some real financial issues here which will take time for you to analyse, and this is best carried out by you, at least initially. It is important not only that you are informed of the process but also that you are aware of your financial position now and into the future.

Motivation

You need a deal that keeps you motivated. The person most often quoted in relation to motivation is Abraham Maslow. Maslow stated that humans are driven by five needs, and he placed them in a hierarchy: the lower-grade needs must be satisfied first; and once they are met we move on to satisfying our higher-grade needs. The first three needs are:

1. **Physiological** needs, such as air, food, drink and shelter
2. **Safety** needs, such as security, protection, order, law and stability in our life
3. **Social** needs, such as belonging, work, group, family and relationships

Not being able to achieve these first three needs will have a detrimental impact on you and your family's lives. When preparing your financial budgets you should ensure that these basic needs are catered for. Starting from the position that you must pay a set amount to your bank and make the rest of the budget fit may lead you to neglect these needs and make an unworkable deal.

When these needs are fulfilled we can strive for the higher-grade needs:

4. **Self-esteem** needs, such as achievement, independence and status
5. **Self-actualisation** needs, such as realising our personal potential and self-fulfilment

Again, if you do not set the correct base with the first three needs you will struggle to motivate yourself to get out of your difficulties. In fairness to your lender, they will recognise your need for a reasonable living standard to satisfy your basic needs, and while they will examine your budgets carefully they will make allowance for what are termed 'priority debts'. These are debts which if not paid can lead to you losing one or more of the following:

- **Your family home:** mortgage or rental payments
- **Your liberty:** tax payments; child support
- **Utilities:** gas, electricity, etc. necessary for personal comfort
- **Essentials:** travel to work; household items such as furniture

You will realise from the above that these coincide somewhat with Maslow's first three needs – there are no luxuries involved.

What Is Your Goal?

You need to make a decision on your goal in negotiating with your lender.

The motivational lesson above may not be very motivating when you consider that your lender will more than likely be negotiating an existence for you at the lower end of Maslow's motivational scale. You will have higher aspirations for your future. Accordingly, when approaching any resolution to your problem it is important to consider what your goal is. This might be:

- Achieving debt forgiveness
- Maintaining an acceptable lifestyle
- Reducing financial risk for your dependants
- Ensuring a comfortable retirement in the longer term
- A combination of all of these

If we look briefly at each of these you will realise that before you enter serious negotiations with your lender it is best to take a holistic approach to your finances and your plans.

Debt Forgiveness

If you achieve debt forgiveness, you may still, for many years, have a lifestyle that you may not find acceptable and that may leave little money to plan adequately for your retirement. Your lender, if considering debt forgiveness, is likely to seek as low a write-down as is compatible with you being able to service the new loan. This will mean very little room for luxuries in your budget.

Lenders may, under their long-term strategies, seek to hold a portion of the debt in abeyance – or warehoused – in the hope that they can achieve some recovery on this at a later date. So seeking debt forgiveness may not result in a better lifestyle unless you achieve a permanent reduction in your debt with no claw-back (refundable money) option from your lender at a later date. In addition, the size of the new mortgage must enable an acceptable living standard combined with an ability to make plans for retirement.

Maintaining an Acceptable Lifestyle

Maintaining an acceptable lifestyle may prove easier if you are prepared to accept less debt forgiveness or just debt deferment. It will also rely on the prospect of you being able to return to work in the near term, with full recovery of your loan being a real prospect for your lender. If your case is particularly difficult, with an unsustainable mortgage and negative equity, the sale of the property in return for significant debt forgiveness may be the only way to get your life back. As pointed out in earlier chapters, the mortgage arrears process supports you staying in your home, so you will have plenty of time to consider this option.

Reducing Financial Risk for Your Dependants

When you mention life insurance to most people, they run for cover in the belief that you are just trying to make money out of them. The average life expectancy of people in Ireland is mid-seventies for men and early eighties for women, so you may think that life cover is a waste of money. However, a lack of adequate life cover can expose your dependants to financial risk.

It is a legal requirement to have life cover (or mortgage protection, as it is called) on your family home so that in the event of your untimely death your dependants will be relieved of the burden of the mortgage payments. There are two other areas that are worth considering as part of your financial plan and outgoings when preparing your budgets:

1. As there is no legal requirement to have life cover on investment properties, there is a strong possibility that in many cases there is no adequate risk management in place in case of death. The assumption in the past was that the property value would repay the debt and that the rental income could service the debt in the meantime. Both assumptions may no longer be valid, and many households could be carrying an additional financial risk.
2. The level of life cover needed to cover annual costs in the event of the death of the prime earner or earners needs to be assessed in any financial plan for the future, even if debt servicing is a problem.

Case Study

Jack and Maura are married with three children aged 10 to 15. Maura works in the home. Jack is in salaried employment but has experienced a 25 per cent salary reduction in the past year and rental reductions on three investment properties purchased during the boom years.

All loans are in the names of Jack and Maura, so they are jointly liable for the debt. Should Jack pass away Maura will receive an annual payment from both the state and Jack's pension scheme. They reviewed their financial exposure in the event of the untimely death of one of them and revealed the following:

- The family home is fully insured and will be repaid. It is valued at €400,000.
- The investment properties have no insurance cover and are in negative equity of €500,000.
- In addition to an annual payment to Maura on Jack's death, she will receive a death in service payment of €180,000.
- Maura would be unable to work after Jack's death until the children have completed college. The shortfall in funding the family budget over the next ten years is estimated at €25,000 per year.
- If Maura were to die, Jack would receive no money as her life is not insured. He estimates a family budget shortfall of €40,000 per year.

The above simplified situation merely points out some of the financial risk elements that need to be considered in your proposal to resolve your debt problem. As you can see from the above, as Maura is jointly responsible for the investment property loans, she will retain this debt should Jack die.

Once you start discussing debt resolution you should request a meeting with one of your lender's financial advisers to establish gaps in your life cover and seek to close, at the lowest cost, any financial risk you have. The cost of new life cover should be included in your budget.

Do Not Forget About Retirement

Any consideration of your financial position now must look far enough ahead to your retirement years. In the boom years everything looked rosy and a good retirement seemed assured. We are now experiencing lower or stagnant incomes with little prospect of meaningful increases in the next five to seven years. Many companies that provide pension benefits are now looking to modify their schemes and are asking their employees to take more of the risk. Higher taxes, lower social benefits and fewer free services can be expected in the future.

Any deal you seek to do on your debt must focus not only on how it helps you now but also on how it helps you in the future. Having a warehoused loan at 65 years of age is only worth considering if the deal is right and you can have an acceptable retirement.

Remember to Calculate Your Lifetime Earnings

In Chapter 4 we looked at lifetime earnings to encourage you to look at your financial future as a whole and not just the particular difficulty you have at present. It can provide more clarity on how you might resolve the problem in the context of having a reasonable living standard and an acceptable retirement. Most of us can predict this with some accuracy. Even if you are out of work at present, making some estimates of future earnings can be useful when constructing your plan.

Looking back to the example of Patrick and Kate in Chapter 4 (page 68), they worked out that their total lifetime income would be €3,130,000. While this figure looks large, it is an estimated total fund available to Patrick and Kate over a 45-year period. We have not included any outgoings such as mortgage payments. If we assume that Patrick has a mortgage of €700,000 and wishes to repay this over the 25 years to age 65 the impact on his lifetime earnings fund will be as follows:

Lifetime earnings to age 65 (based on €54,000 per year at 3% growth)	€1,970,000
Total mortgage repayments (€44,000 per year)	€1,100,000
Net earnings available to age 65	€870,000
Average available per year to age 65	€34,800

From this Patrick has to accommodate:

- An acceptable lifestyle for him and his family from now until retirement
- Education and other expenses for his children

However, whilst Patrick may be able to accommodate his plans over his lifetime, he will be unable to comfortably pay the annual payments of €44,000 at present, as his net salary is currently €54,000. A deal based on paying a portion of his disposable income (say 40 per cent) may be the way to go to achieve his goal of being debt free at age 65.

The above approach may seem simplistic, but it is provided to get you to focus on the total amount of money you will have available over your remaining lifetime and how you need to use it. There is little point in agreeing to a deal that forces you to rely on other short-term finance sources such as credit cards to pay for day-to-day expenses and gets you into further difficulty.

Patrick may have to look at a combination of asset sales, debt deferment and a lump sum payment from his retirement fund to maintain an acceptable lifestyle now.

So in structuring a deal with your lender you would do well to consider the long term and, depending on your debt position and your ability to service your debt, seek to achieve a deal that satisfies your overall goals. This may involve selling assets, deferring debt, interest forgiveness or debt forgiveness and commitments around partial lump-sum payments.

What Does Your Financial Future Look Like?

What we are looking to do here is to establish, after analysing all your income and outgoings, what net cash is available to develop your financial plan for the future. If this is insufficient and there are assets available (even those in negative equity) you may consider selling these as part of your proposal.

How Much Do You Currently Earn?

Start with your basic household budget. This will show you how much you are earning, how much you are spending and whether there is anything left over to provide for the future. Once you have finished this exercise you will have a clearer understanding of your financial position, and it will highlight some areas that you may have to change. It is also important that you take into account joint income and expenditures if you operate household budgets with your spouse or partner.

Try not to overestimate or underestimate your income and spending, and use accurate figures from household bills as far as possible. Remember, you are looking to achieve an accurate picture, not delude yourself into thinking you have a massive surplus if that is not the case. Your lender will not seek to add items to your budget if they are not essential to your basic living.

If there are discretionary expenses, such as meals out, which have become regular expenses, make sure you include them, at least initially. You can take them out as you formulate your proposal, but it is important to consciously reduce expenditure, together with all those affected by the cuts, as you and they will have to live with them going forward.

Also allow for holidays, Christmases and birthdays. You may have to take some of these out or pare back your expectations later, but now is not the time to exclude reasonable expenses that will help you cope with the situation you are in.

If you are honest in compiling your budget, you will be able to see what your finances will be like in the future based on your current lifestyle, and you will be able to carry out your own review of where savings are possible while retaining an acceptable living standard. You will need to have this clearly in your mind when you meet with your lender regarding your current financial difficulties.

Below is a budget format I like to use. It seeks to identify the areas where spending is necessary and where cutbacks may need to be considered. It is useful for those people experiencing financial difficulties and also for those seeking to carry out a financial planning exercise.

Sample Budget

Financial Category	Monthly Figures
Income	
Salary	
Salary of spouse/partner	
State payments	
Annual bonus (if applicable)	
Unearned income (bank interest, dividends, etc.)	
Total Income (A)	*This line highlights income from all sources and is the amount you have to deal with your financial commitments.*
Expenses	
Food	
Life assurance (mortgage protection) and health insurance	
Motor expenses	
Child costs, education	
Medical expenses	

(Continued)

Sample Budget (*Continued*)

Financial Category	Monthly Figures
Household – electricity/TV/ phone, etc.	
Other	
Sub-Total: Necessary Expenses (B)	*This represents all the expenses you must incur to have a basic standard of living.*
Discretionary Spending	
Entertainment	
Club membership	
Holidays	
Sub-Total: Discretionary Expenses (C)	*This is the total of expenses, some of which may be necessary but have a discretionary element. These are likely to be the ones your lender may look to restrict.*
Net Cash to Service Your Financial Commitments (E) = (A–(B+C))	*These are the funds you will have to service your financial commitments and reduce your financial risk through additional life cover.*
Financial Commitments	
Mortgage payments	
Investment property payments	
Car loan repayments	
Credit card repayments	
Personal loan repayments	
Life cover – additional	

(*Continued*)

Sample Budget (*Continued*)

Financial Category	Monthly Figures
Total Financial Commitments (F)	*This represents your total financial commitments as they currently stand; it may also include additional insurances beyond mortgage protection to cover investment properties and living expenses.*
Surplus (Deficit) Available for Savings, Investments and Retirement Planning (E–F)	*This is the surplus available to cover future expenses, such as college fees and retirement benefits.*

What we are looking to do here is to establish, after analysing all your income and outgoings, what net cash is available to develop your financial plan for the future. The reason for this approach is that your financial future is effectively a trade-off between what you can afford to have now (entertainment, holidays, etc.) and the lifestyle you want in retirement. The equation works out like this:

Total Income	Less	Equals
From salary and supports	Essential, discretionary and financial expenses	Money to create your retirement plan

In order to increase the money available, you can either focus on the Total Income box and try to improve this or look critically at the Total Expenses box and cut back. The approach you take or the options available to you will depend on what stage you are at in your life cycle, how much money you have already provided for your retirement, and your view on what constitutes a reasonable lifestyle now and in retirement. Increasing your total income will depend on:

- Your current income and prospects for income growth through promotion or career change
- If you are currently out of work, the likelihood of gaining work and at what salary level

If the net sum available looks low or negative, do not get despondent: a significant part of your financial future may already have been taken care of without you necessarily being fully aware of it, for example:

- Many people are in a company pension scheme that provides an income on retirement. Some of these schemes also have an element of life cover. So your difficulty may be related to your short-term cash position, which is what requires attention now.
- As mentioned previously, if you have a mortgage you more than likely have mortgage protection. Therefore, the exercise now is to see what extras you currently need to cover such things as negative equity while you work out a deal with your lender.

If you have a financial problem that is current and is also bleak in terms of your retirement prospects, you may have to look at a debt forgiveness option to rebalance that situation. This will mean either negotiating a restructured deal involving sufficient debt forgiveness to provide a reasonable lifestyle now and in retirement, or looking to the remedies I will discuss in Parts III and IV of this book.

How Much Are You Worth?

Having looked at your monthly cash flow, we now turn to your personal balance sheet. This is basically an assessment of all your assets and the debt associated with them. Using the table below you can list all your assets in the first column and place the value of those assets in the second column. The third column outlines the borrowing attached to each asset. The total row at the end will indicate whether you have positive overall equity or negative equity.

Personal Balance Sheet

Assets	Value	Liability (Borrowings)	Total
Family home			
Investment property 1			
Investment property 2			
Home contents			
Savings			
Other investments			
Jewellery			
Cars			
Value of pension			
Other			
Total			

How do I use this information?

The information dealt with in this chapter will be required by your financial adviser or a personal insolvency practitioner and, as we saw in Chapter 6, your lender has a standard financial statement for you to complete.

The standard financial statement is a lengthy form and you might be tempted to just quickly fill it out and hand it to your lender. However, the purpose of what we have outlined in this chapter is to get you active in the solution to your problem. Take the time to assess your position. This will help you formulate your approach to your problem.

> **Remember:** once your lender has catered for 'priority debts' they will be looking to maximise the recovery of their mortgage or other loan over time.

Your lender is focused on their problem, which is the recovery of loans within the context of the mortgage arrears and insolvency processes. You need to take a longer-term view of your financial situation so that the process gets you an acceptable result. The analysis above will give you an initial feel for the following questions, which you can then discuss with an adviser or insolvency practitioner:

- If your monthly cash flow is negative and you cannot pay your mortgage, is it a long-term problem or will it resolve itself over two to five years? Some of the debts you owe may be short term, and if you are allowed to clear them you may be able to return to mortgage payments in two to five years. If not, you may be insolvent.
- What asset(s) or property can be sold, and how will this alter the financial picture? If an element of debt forgiveness is available, will this help? How much is needed?
- Are you in serious negative equity, where significant debt forgiveness is the only solution?
- How is your retirement plan looking at this point, and will you be in a position to have an acceptable retirement?

Should I use a financial adviser?

If you have done your financial analysis thoroughly you will have a fair idea of the answer to this question. If you are not confident that you can resolve the problem it makes sense to have a financial adviser look at your case and perhaps represent you in negotiations with your lender.

If you suspect that you are insolvent and therefore qualify for a personal insolvency solution, it may save money to consult a practitioner who can bring you all the way to this process.

SUMMARY

Analysis of your financial position is perhaps the most crucial part of the process for you. All the processes for resolving the personal debt and mortgage arrears crisis are in place but are based on the principle that only the people who cannot afford to pay get help. If you require and deserve help you will have to prove it, and the best way of doing this is with an accurate assessment of your financial situation. Accuracy, together with transparency, is vital to gain trust; and, as solutions at the personal insolvency level are based on a sworn statement of income, any omissions could undermine your deal.

I have suggested that you take a holistic and long-term view of your situation, but your lender will not necessarily be focused on this. However, although many people may feel that they will work the problem out over their lifetime you must be sure that you can, and the best way to do this is to do the figures.

Remember, while you may be optimistic or avoiding a critical analysis of your situation, the test as to whether you are insolvent and eligible to apply for personal insolvency only requires your personal insolvency practitioner to take a five-year view.

Key Points in this Chapter

1. We have pointed out a number of times in this book that an accurate assessment of your financial position is the corner-stone of any debt resolution plan.
2. Your lender will be mainly concerned with achieving debt repayment, and, while this is your objective too, you also have to take a more holistic look at your current and future financial position.
3. The living standard afforded you under any of the initial debt resolution processes will be adequate at best and could remain so for many years unless your financial circumstances change sufficiently.
4. You need to consider the financial risks associated with your current borrowing and what would happen if you died. Will the risk remain with your spouse or partner?
5. Completing a full and accurate budget is essential, and it is best to start with all your current spending and then look to economise, rather than starting with mortgage payments and leaving essentials out.
6. Ensure that your budget includes all expenses that must be incurred – it will be too late to alter it after the deal is done with your lender. Your lender will not be looking to add expenditure to your budget.
7. Review your asset and debt position. If you decide to go down the insolvency or bankruptcy route to resolve your debt problem, you will have to prove that you are insolvent.
8. Do not be afraid to either consult an independent financial adviser or to use your lender's personal advisers to help you assess your financial position regarding insurances and finan-cial risk.
9. Stay focused on a holistic solution to your problem rather than a short-term solution.
10. You may have goals and ambitions for a lifestyle that now seem unlikely to happen, given the circumstances, but this is not the time to lose sight of them.

8

How Your Lender Assesses Your Case

Don't bargain yourself down before you get to the table.
**Carol Frohlinger, US author, speaker and cofounder of
Negotiating Women, Inc.**

Once you have informed your lender of your problem and
provided your financial information, the process of assessment and resolution will begin. It is likely that once you
engage in the process some short-term relief will be quite
easily achieved, at least in most cases. This will allow both
parties to begin the process and focus on the solution.

If you still have equity in your house, can service the interest and there is a reasonable prospect of a return to normal
repayments, some latitude for six to twelve months would
seem achievable. If your problem is more severe – negative
equity, inability to pay interest and no clarity as to when
the full repayments can restart – the conversation with your
lender may be more intense.

Even if your lender views the sale of the property as the
outcome, they are likely to provide initial relief until they see
how things develop. In fact, as outlined below, the Code of
Conduct on Mortgage Arrears states that all options must be
explored, including deferring payment of all or part of the
instalment repayments for a period. The Code states:

A lender must explore all options for alternative repayment arrangements, when considering a MARP case, in order to determine which options are viable for each particular case. Such alternative repayment arrangements must include:

(a) an interest-only arrangement for a specified period;
(b) an arrangement to pay interest and part of the normal capital element for a specified period;
(c) deferring payment of all or part of the instalment repayment for a period;
(d) extending the term of the mortgage;
(e) changing the type of the mortgage, except in the case of tracker mortgages;
(f) capitalising the arrears and interest; and
(g) any voluntary scheme to which the lender has signed up e.g. Deferred Interest Scheme.

Code of Conduct on Mortgage Arrears 2010
(Chapter 3, Clause 33)

Step 3: Assessment

This step involves your plans being assessed by your lender. You may initially deal with the local branch of your lender, but the assessment will be carried out by the arrears support unit (ASU). This is a specialist unit which the Code requires the lender to set up to deal with customers with mortgage arrears. The ASU will assess your standard financial statement and may seek supporting documentation for some items. They are required under the Code to examine each case on its individual merits. A lender's ASU must base its assessment of your case on your full circumstances, including:

- Your personal circumstances
- Your overall indebtedness
- The information you provide in the standard financial statement

- Your current repayment capacity
- Your previous payment history

Your lender must distinguish between customers who have the ability to pay and those who will not pay. Accordingly their assessment will be thorough. As I have said before, the Code and the structure it has put in place will help reach an acceptable solution, but your lender will not be a pushover and will be forensic in their analysis of your position.

However, there is no need to be intimidated by this stage. If you use the approach recommended in this book, you will be more than capable of presenting a good and accurate case of your financial position to your lender. You will also be able to outline a proposal as to how your current situation can be resolved.

You may, for instance, be in this position due to unemployment, so you need to assess the prospects for your trade or profession and the likelihood of employment in the short term. The relief you are looking for is something that will take you to a place where you can resume payments.

You may, of course, be in much more difficulty with a mortgage payment and in a situation where a resolution is unlikely to be achievable in the short to medium term. This may perhaps be due to unemployment, compounded by the fact that a return to work in your trade or profession will result in a much lower income. Other situations, such as illness, can affect your ability to repay your mortgage.

The essential point here is that you must try to assess your ability to repay your mortgage in the medium to long term.

Armed with the financial and other information you have provided, your lender will assess the likelihood of you being in a position to make capital and interest payments at present and also at some future date. Initially they will be seeking to distinguish between customers who cannot pay and those who will not pay.

Once the assessment is complete, your lender will propose a solution. As outlined above, there are a number of options they must look at and discuss with you.

Step 4: Resolution

Your lender's proposed resolution is another key part of the process. You may be tempted to accept anything they propose and struggle to make it work, but you should give this part of the process serious consideration. If you have done your work thoroughly, as outlined in this book, you will have made your own accurate assessment of what is achievable. Hopefully, your lender will agree. If the proposal put forward by your lender is different from what you are proposing, you need to consider whether this is acceptable to you. You need to be sure that you can keep to what is agreed and cope with the impact it will have on your lifestyle.

Some people may approach the problem, and the financial information, from the viewpoint that their current lifestyle must be maintained. Your lender, for their part, may feel that if you make certain cutbacks you could contribute more to your mortgage payments. This is why, as pointed out in Chapter 7, it is vital to be scrupulously accurate in preparing your financial information. This information will be scrutinised by your lender for possible cutbacks, savings and the restructuring of other lenders' loans.

Also remember that it is the information in your financial statement that will form the basis of the deal you agree with your lender. Your lender will want to help; however, they will be looking for as large a mortgage contribution as possible. The standard financial statement form will outline most of the expenses and costs you need to take into account, but do make sure that you include absolutely everything. The reason for this is that only you know the full extent of your living costs, and after negotiations with your lender you will be expected to keep to the deal. You have to forensically examine your expenses because if you leave out items that must be incurred, you will put pressure on your finances as you struggle to maintain your new deal with your lender.

Your lender will base their assessment on a number of factors. First, they will look at your personal circumstances as you have presented them. Then they will look at your overall indebtedness – basically, loans you have with them and with other lenders, credit cards, store cards, etc. They will review in detail the financial information you provided and may have their own view on particular expense levels. They will review your previous repayment track records and look at your current repayment capacity.

The key points to remember are:

- Accurately assess your position and make sure all expenses are covered.
- Be realistic about how much money you need to support an acceptable lifestyle.
- Present yourself well and confidently, particularly if you have a good track record with the lender.

All this will lead to a robust assessment, taking in all the elements of current debts, your circumstances and your ability to pay. Once your lender has completed their assessment they will have to look at all options for an alternative repayment arrangement.

When considering a case under MARP, your lender must consider a number of possible alternative arrangements outlined in the Code, as follows:

- An interest-only arrangement for a specified period. This involves your lender foregoing capital payments for a period of time, usually six to twelve months initially. There will be no reduction in your mortgage loan during this period.
- An arrangement to pay interest and part of the normal capital element for a specified period. This solution provides

that you make interest payments and some element of capital payment. Your mortgage will reduce by the amount of capital payments made.

- Deferring payment of all or part of the instalment repayment for a period. This will result in your mortgage loan increasing by the amount of deferred interest.
- Extending the term of the mortgage. As mortgages are normally extended to age 65 or, in some cases, 70, you may be able to reschedule the repayment period.
- Changing the type of the mortgage, except in the case of tracker mortgages.
- Capitalising the arrears and interest. This involves adding the current arrears and interest to the mortgage until you are in a position to recommence payments of interest and, hopefully, capital. Your mortgage loan will increase by the interest amount capitalised to the account.
- Any voluntary scheme to which the lender has signed up, e.g. a deferred interest scheme.

You will notice from the above solutions that there is no reduction in your liability, and in some cases it will increase until you start payments again. In Part III we will be looking at other options being introduced by lenders where a longer-term view is being taken. In Part IV we will look at how legislation on insolvency and even bankruptcy can help you resolve your particular situation, either as a chosen solution or as a negotiating stance with your lender.

Finally, it is important to know that while your lender must *consider* such arrangements, they are not obliged to *offer* you one. This is what makes the financial information stage and your ability to present your case so important.

Now we will look at the final stage in MARP, though if the resolution proposed is not acceptable and agreement cannot be reached with your lender, it is not necessarily the end of your negotiation.

Step 5: Appeals

Do you need to appeal? As already stated, the Code is designed to provide a process for you and your lender to resolve your financial difficulties in a mutually satisfactory way. Whether you get an acceptable result will very much depend on the earlier stages of the process and how successfully you presented your case.

However, this does not mean that your lender will automatically go with your preferred option. There will be a fair element of negotiation with your lender as they are looking to recover all the money they have lent, and they are not bound to offer a solution; however, they are unlikely to take action prematurely.

If you cannot adhere to the original terms of the mortgage, your lender will consider as their best option loan solutions that maintain all the debt in place with no debt forgiveness. This means that, while you may gain a cash flow benefit from a new arrangement, you will continue to be fully liable for all the debt.

They may also propose an initial short-term solution for perhaps twelve months in the hope that your financial situation improves. This may be all you need, but, as we explained in Chapter 7, you have to have an acceptable living standard both now and into the future.

In the event that you are unhappy with the lender's proposal you can appeal the decision to your lender's appeals board – all lenders must have an appeals body. The Code states:

A lender must allow the borrower a reasonable period of time to consider submitting an appeal to the Appeals Board, which must be at least 20 business days from the date he/she received notification of the decision of the lender's ASU.

Code of Conduct on Mortgage Arrears 2010
(Chapter 3, Clause 45)

127

So if your lender offers a proposal you find unacceptable you can appeal the decision. This may help you both achieve an improvement in the deal proposed and also allow you to reflect on whether you could make the deal work. You can take an appeal on any of the following grounds:

- Your lender's decision on your case
- How your lender treated you under MARP
- If you feel that your lender has not complied with any of the requirements under the Code of Conduct on Mortgage Arrears

You must submit your appeal within twenty business days of receiving the lender's decision on your case. If you are not happy with the outcome of the appeal you can make a complaint to the Financial Services Ombudsman.

It is clear from what we have just outlined that reaching a mutual and acceptable agreement is the best way forward. You should also realise that there is a lot in your favour and your lender will be seeking an amicable result.

You also now know that the process from the day you go into arrears until the unthinkable event of losing your house is a long one. It is a long process because your lender will want to exhaust all avenues to find a solution. For your part, it is important that you remain in negotiation and engaged with your lender.

To achieve the best result you must do your homework well, understand your financial position, be prepared to present your case and stay calm and confident that you can achieve the result.

What if the lender wants to repossess my home?

In relation to house repossessions, the lender is required to make every reasonable attempt to agree an alternative arrangement with you or your nominated representative before applying to the court to commence legal action for repossession.

The importance of co-operating with your lender cannot be overstated: do not ignore the problem or your lender. Once you are co-operating your lender must wait at least twelve months from the day you were classified as in need of the resolution process before applying to the courts to commence legal action. The Code states:

> Where a borrower co-operates with the lender, the lender must wait at least twelve months from the date the borrower is classified as a MARP case (i.e. day 31), before applying to the courts to commence legal action for repossession of a borrower's primary residence.

The twelve-month period commences on day 31 but does not include:

- Any time period during which the borrower is complying with the terms of any alternative repayment arrangement agreed with the lender
- Any time period during which an appeal by the borrower is being processed by the lender's Appeals Board
- Any time period during which the borrower can consider whether or not they wish to make an appeal on the decision of the ASU
- Any time period during which a complaint against the lender regarding any aspect of this Code is being processed by the Financial Services Ombudsman's office and
- For pre-arrears cases, the time period between the first contact by the borrower in relation to a pre-arrears situation and an alternative repayment arrangement being put in place

Taken from the Code of Conduct on Mortgage Arrears 2010
(Chapter 3, Clause 47)

The twelve-month period excludes any time during which you were complying with any alternative arrangement agreed with the lender, any time in which you were engaged in an appeals process, or any time you spent considering entering into an appeals process. The new consultation process on MARP will consider the appropriate notice period prior to repossession proceedings commencing in cases where an offer of support is not provided by your lender.

So the central point here is that there is a significant amount of time during which your lender cannot make a move to repossess your house, and this time can be used productively to do an acceptable deal and also to deal with your financial position.

SUMMARY

Understanding how your lender assesses your case is central to achieving the desired result. If you get a result you are happy with at the MARP level you will need to go no further. However, an acceptable result will depend on you being an active participant in the process and being realistic about what you can afford to pay and what is achievable.

Prepare your financial information accurately and be sure to include all necessary expenses. Be prepared to make a strong case if your lender is looking for unreasonable cuts. Consider using an adviser if the solution proposed is unacceptable or if you are intimidated by the process. Include the cost of this in your budget.

Remember, you can appeal any decision. At a minimum this will provide a cooling-off period to allow you to consider your options and think about whether, with a further adjustment, your lender's proposal may be workable. Your lender cannot make a move to repossess your home during this period.

You need to take a rational approach to your problem – which is difficult during troubled times – and an accurate assessment of your situation. If you do not get what you feel you need or can work with, there are other options available to you, and these will be discussed in Parts III and IV of the book.

Key Points in this Chapter

1. Assessment and resolution are the objectives of MARP. These are based on an accurate understanding of your financial position.
2. It is your responsibility to ensure that you present your lender with an accurate picture of your financial situation now and into the future.
3. Your lender will forensically examine your financial details during the assessment, so be prepared to defend expenditures that are absolutely necessary.
4. The resolution to your problem must be negotiated, and proper preparation is required to achieve your desired result.
5. Make sure that you are happy with and can keep to any deal proposed – you may have to live with it for many years.
6. If your case is very serious and you need debt or interest forgiveness, talk to a professional adviser.
7. Remember that there are other long-term options available (see Parts III and IV).
8. Keeping the communication lines open and remaining in the process will help to keep you in your house for longer.

Part III

Mortgage Arrears Resolution Strategy (MARS): Your Lender's Longer-Term Solutions to Mortgage Arrears

In this part I will outline the Mortgage Arrears Resolution Strategy (MARS), which is designed to tackle long-term unsustainable mortgages in arrears. I will provide an overview of the solutions MARS offers to give you a flavour of whether they can help you resolve your mortgage difficulties.

I will then provide a detailed review of each strategy with worked examples and insights into how they can be adapted to find a workable solution.

As buy-to-let mortgages do not have the protection of the MARP process, Chapter 11 is devoted to considering how you might address mortgage arrears on these loans.

9

Longer-Term Solutions: An Overview

*During a negotiation, it would be wise not to take
anything personally. If you leave personalities out of it,
you will be able to see opportunities more objectively.*
Brian Koslow, US financial trainer and coach

With the economic climate's failure to improve, it has
become clear that some of the Level 1 mortgage loan modifications are too short term. In many cases, at the end of this
initial loan modification period mortgage holders are unable
to return to the original terms of their loan agreement. This
has prompted a move by the Central Bank and lenders to
look at more long-term loan modifications.

Case Study

Liam and Fiona have a mortgage of €350,000 over 25 years
with monthly payments of €1,850. Liam is no longer working
and is unlikely to return to work any time soon.

Fiona works in sales and has experienced a significant
drop in income. It is unlikely that Liam and Fiona's financial position will improve until there is a major uplift in the
economy.

After twelve months on one of the short-term solutions
(they had been paying interest only at €1,160 per month) it
is now clear that they need a longer-term solution to their
problem.

Many people are finding themselves in a position similar to Liam and Fiona's. Having spent six, twelve or eighteen months on short-term solutions they can see no immediate release from their financial difficulties. Some people may need more than a pick-up in the economy to be in a position to finance the high cost of the property they purchased during the boom years, not to mention other needs such as their children's education and retirement funding.

The reasons for their difficulty can be many and varied, including:

- A drop in salaries due to the loss of performance-related pay or bonuses
- Salary and wage cuts resulting from the market downturn
- The prospect that their current salary level is likely to stay the same for many years
- A permanent reduction in take-home pay as a result of higher taxes and other government-enforced charges
- A move to lower-paid employment following redundancy

In many cases the people affected by events like these will not see a return to the disposable income they enjoyed prior to the downturn. If their commitments are high, having been based on their historical disposable income, they may now find themselves in difficulties.

There can also be other reasons for a person's difficulties, which may be related to the economy or accentuated by the downturn. Examples include:

- Relationship breakdown
- Death of a family member who contributed economically to the household budget
- Maternity leave, which can cause a temporary problem or increase long-term costs through childcare expenses
- The need for one spouse or partner to return to full-time education as a solution to improving the long-term financial position

Present Debt and Commitments

The financial expenditure witnessed during the Celtic Tiger years not only impacted house prices but also led to people making decisions that will have a financial impact for many years to come. Many of us spent money on consumer goods such as cars, house extensions or club memberships and financed these purchases on a short-term basis in the anticipation of continued salary increases. Other readily available sources of finance were used to finance day-to-day lifestyles, which has led to increases in credit card debt.

What Is the Solution?

The solution is for the lender to look holistically at the problems facing their customers and put in place a solution that extends over a number of years rather than just six to twelve months. The new solution will be reviewed annually, or more frequently if circumstances change. From the customer's point of view this may be a solution that is more workable and less stressful.

In some cases it may involve providing latitude to allow the borrower to pay off the short-term loans, such as personal and credit card debts, and then return to normal mortgage payments. In others the problem may be more severe, and the solution may have to be in place for some time, with no certainty as to when it will end.

A Word of Warning

The initial mortgage arrears solutions, such as interest-only payments, and the new longer-term Mortgage Arrears Resolution Strategy (MARS) are part of the same process under the Code of Conduct on Mortgage Arrears. I have described them as Level 1 and Level 2 because MARS represents a move to longer-term solutions.

In many cases these will suit individuals as the basis of a permanent way of dealing with their financial problem. In other cases
they will represent a deferment of the debt, and this may not be
what is needed. Not only may it not be what you need, but you
may also have better options available to you if you fit the criteria
for debt forgiveness.

What Are the Criteria for Debt Forgiveness?

I have stated a number of times that there is no policy for
general debt forgiveness; there is no plan to actively assess
each case and decide whether debt forgiveness should be
given; and there is no form to be filled out and assessed for
debt forgiveness.

In reality there are criteria, but not at Level 1 and 2 solutions. At these levels, if you want to achieve debt forgiveness
it will have to be negotiated. Debt forgiveness is more likely
at the Level 3 and Level 4 solutions of insolvency and bankruptcy – if you meet the criteria and are prepared to follow
the process.

As we shall see in Part IV on personal insolvency, to
achieve the benefit of the personal insolvency process you
must be certified by your personal insolvency practitioner
to be financially insolvent and also likely to remain that way
for five years. There are a number of rules to comply with,
which your personal insolvency practitioner will assess
and explain. The important point here is that if you cannot
live with the MARS options presented by your lender, you
should consider taking professional advice before signing
any new agreement.

For bankruptcy there are also criteria you must meet,
which must be proved to a court, but, subject to satisfying
these criteria, you may achieve debt forgiveness.

Is debt forgiveness likely under MARS?

We will outline the three solutions covered by MARS shortly and go into them in more detail in the next chapter. MARS does not automatically include debt forgiveness as part of the deal, so achieving this outcome will require much negotiation. This is why I have mentioned above that debt forgiveness is possible, but in most circumstances this is by using either the personal insolvency or bankruptcy process, in which it is the prime objective of the process.

Doing the Deal with Your Lender

As you move from your lender's initial short-term loan modifications, you need to stay focused on a solution that is right for you. This solution will not be easily achieved, and it takes time, patience and knowledge of your financial position to be successful. If you believe your case is strong it may be wise to get professional advice and representation at the early stage of the process.

Documents provided by your lender will suggest that you should consider independent advice or consult the Money Advice and Budgeting Service (MABS). This covers your lender's legal position and their duties to advise you. However, it is good advice, which is worth considering.

If you are in discussions with your lender on a longer-term loan modification it is important that you ensure it fits with your own financial assessment of your position. I continue to stress the need to examine your financial position and know both what you want to achieve and how far you will go to achieve it. The reasons for this are:

- Your lender does not have to offer you any deal.
- If you do not properly assess your position, your lender may feel that they have the upper hand and that you are likely to accept what is offered and go no further.

- If you reach this point you will either have to sign what is offered or move to the next process. It is important that you know what this entails and what the implications are for you.
- Some people may just accept what is offered, which gives immediate relief as they do not want the aggravation of non-acceptance.

The Long-Term Solutions

Three solutions have been proposed under MARS to provide longer-term relief, as follows:

1. **Trade-down mortgage** – This will involve selling your current home as part of any arrangement and moving to a house which achieves a reduction in your debt to an amount you can repay over a reasonable period (usually to age 65).
2. **Split mortgage** – This will involve the warehousing or parking of an element of your debt and repaying the balance over an agreed period. The warehoused portion is reintroduced as your repayment ability improves.
3. **Mortgage to rent** – This is a government scheme under which you give up your house and rent it back from a housing agency. As the housing agency will purchase your house from your lender at market value there may be residual debt left over if the purchase price is less than the loan. How you deal with this residual debt is between you and your lender.

These solutions continue the emphasis on keeping people in their homes while providing for a reasonable standard of living. The object of each alternative solution is to provide what is termed an 'affordability gain' by warehousing an element of the loan, trading down to a different house or selling the house and renting it back. Neither debt forgiveness nor interest forgiveness is a standard feature of any of the processes, but may feature if negotiated by you or your adviser.

In the case of a split mortgage and a mortgage to rent, you stay in your current house. However, with the trade-down mortgage you move to another property. The affordability gain refers to the fact that you can now afford the new mortgage level.

As each individual's case is different, we cannot cover all examples here, but the next chapter will give a flavour of what is proposed in each option.

Do any of the three long-term solutions provide debt forgiveness?

Everybody's situation is different, and your lender will work on a case-by-case basis. Debt forgiveness could be a part of any solution if you or your adviser can negotiate such a result. However, a review of the basic model for each option would suggest that debt forgiveness is not an automatic part of the process. The emphasis is on providing you with a home at a mortgage level that you can service at present while retaining liability for all the debt.

Different lenders may use the new arrangement differently. For instance, it has been reported in the media that some lenders that offer the split mortgage arrangement do not charge interest on the warehoused element of the loan, while others do. While this is interest forgiveness as opposed to writing off the debt, it is a significant concession and one you should look for if you are agreeing to warehouse an element of your mortgage.

The case-by-case approach adopted by lenders means that there is no set formula, but it is reasonable to assume that some debt or interest forgiveness is achievable if your case is strong. So do not count on debt forgiveness here unless you are prepared to present and negotiate your case well.

What are the upsides of these arrangements?

The main upsides are:

- You remain in your home, or one you trade down to, which is the prime objective of the mortgage arrears process.
- You also achieve monthly repayments based on your income, which should be more manageable.

What are the downsides of these arrangements?

The main downsides may be:

- On the face of it you do not receive any debt forgiveness, so your debt level remains high. With a trade-down mortgage you will reduce your debt level. However, you may still have significant negative equity in the new house. With the split mortgage the debt is deferred and may continue to attract interest.
- The arrangements are subject to annual reviews, so if you earn more disposable income your lender will expect you to increase your repayments. This means that you will be constantly reminded of your financial difficulty and may have no clarity as to how you can use additional money earned to secure your financial future.
- The arrangements will have an emphasis on repaying the debt, so negotiations on living expenses may be difficult.
- In the worst case you may get no debt forgiveness, regular assessment of your family budget and a lifestyle that may not be to your liking. This could go on for perhaps 20 to 25 years or until the loan is repaid.

SUMMARY

Lenders now have three further options to provide for longer-term solutions to assist those who have unsustainable mortgages at present. Three options being tested by the lenders are:

1. Trade-down mortgage – you move from your current home to a lower-cost property at a mortgage level that is affordable but that will still be in negative equity.
2. Split mortgage – your lender warehouses or parks an element of your mortgage, and you retain a mortgage which you can service at present.
3. Mortgage to rent – this is a government scheme targeted at lower-income families. To be eligible you must meet certain income and property value criteria. If eligible, you sell your house to a housing agency and rent it from them.

The positive aspects of MARS are that they allow you to retain a family home with a mortgage at an acceptable level and have a reasonable standard of living. There is no automatic debt forgiveness in these arrangements. Debt forgiveness will have to be negotiated.

Entering one of these arrangements requires careful consideration of the long-term impact it will have on your financial life in terms of servicing deferred loans or mortgages with severe negative equity. These considerations need to be weighed against the other options, such as insolvency or bankruptcy, which, though you may not personally want them, may give you a financially better outcome.

Curiously, the MARS solutions may give your lender the best result. Once the negotiation moves beyond MARS an element of control is lost for your lender and perhaps for you. The areas of insolvency and bankruptcy place both a communication and a financial wedge between you and your lender by the introduction of mandatory paid professionals whom you must engage to act on your behalf.

In the next chapter we will go through each of the three solutions in more detail.

Key Points in this Chapter

1. Your lender and the Central Bank recognise that some mortgages are unsustainable at present and have sought to design more long-term solutions.

2. Three options have been proposed and are being tested by the lenders:
   i.   Trade-down mortgage
   ii. Split mortgage
   iii. Mortgage to rent

3. The options are not fixed or prescribed and will be adapted by the lender on a case-by-case basis for individual situations.

4. A trade-down mortgage involves the borrower selling their existing home and moving to a lower-cost property. They will retain the residual debt from the house sale. They will more than likely have substantial negative equity on the new property but an affordable monthly mortgage payment.

5. A split mortgage seeks to help the borrower remain in their current home and split the mortgage into a sustainable repayment portion and a warehoused portion. The warehoused portion may or may not attract interest, depending on the deal you do with your lender.

6. The mortgage-to-rent scheme is a government initiative aimed at people on income levels up to €35,000. The process involves the borrower surrendering possession of their home and the house being purchased by an approved housing body at market rate. Rent is paid to the housing body. The residual debt is subject to an agreed solution between the borrower and the lender.

7. Debt forgiveness is not an automatic feature of any of the three long-term options.

8. The upside of a long-term solution is that you have a longer horizon on your deal, you remain in a home and the monthly payments are sustainable.

9. The downside is that there is no automatic debt forgiveness. You may remain in negative equity and the agreed standard of living may not be to your liking. The agreements are likely to

be reviewed annually with an emphasis on increasing mortgage payments.

10. These solutions will suit some people, and some may just accept them without thinking them through. You must ask yourself whether the upside is sufficient for you to accept one of these arrangements. If not, you may need to consider other solutions.

10

Longer-Term Solutions: Working Examples

The most difficult thing in any negotiation, almost, is making sure that you strip it of the emotion and deal with the facts.
Howard Baker, former US Senator and ambassador to Japan

What I propose to do in this chapter is give you a better feel for the three long-term solutions being tested by your lender.

We have discussed MARP and the five steps in the process. To recap, these are:

- **Step 1: Communication** – Your lender confirms that you come within the MARP process.
- **Step 2: Financial information** – You complete the standard financial statement, which forms the basis of your discussion on mortgage payment modification.
- **Step 3: Assessment** – Your arrears support unit (ASU) assesses your financial position and considers alternative repayment arrangements.
- **Step 4: Resolution** – Your lender proposes a solution based on the assessment of your financial position.
- **Step 5: Appeals** – You have a right of appeal on certain grounds. Also, if you are not satisfied with the lender's internal appeals decision, you may involve the Financial Services Ombudsman.

When you come to Step 4 – resolution – your lender will initially propose one of the following short-term options:

- Interest only
- Interest plus part capital
- Deferring payments
- Extending the term of the mortgage
- Capitalisation of the arrears and interest
- A combination of the options above

These are provided for short periods of time and usually reviewed every six months.

The new longer-term solution recognises that the problem may not be solvable quickly. Three alternative ideas have been introduced:

- Trade-down mortgage
- Split mortgage
- Mortgage to rent

More new options may develop over time, or these three options may be adjusted to suit changing circumstances. We will look at them now, as they currently stand, in more detail.

Trade-Down Mortgage

The trade-down option is designed for those in mortgage difficulties with high value or larger properties. The idea is that they may be able to trade down to a lower-value house and carry the negative equity with them.

Case Study: Trade-Down Mortgage

Brendan and Alice live in a five-bedroom house in a sought-after part of the city. The house is valued at €800,000. However, they have a mortgage on the property of €1,200,000.

In addition, due to their financial circumstances they are unable to service the mortgage repayments on the €1,200,000 loan. Their lender is suggesting a trade-down mortgage as a possible solution.

Brendan and Alice could sell their current house for €800,000, leaving a residual debt of €400,000. To this debt will be added the cost of purchasing a new house (€350,000) which is deemed serviceable at Brendan and Alice's current level of income. If Brendan and Alice agree they will end up with the following reduced debt level:

New house purchase	€350,000
Residential debt from previous mortgage	€400,000
New mortgage over, say, 25 years	€750,000

This €750,000 will be repaid over 25 years as their age profile warrants it and they have sufficient projected income.

The advantage of the arrangement to the lender is that they achieve a reduced mortgage from €1,200,000 to €750,000 now and a sustainable repayment structure which will result in full repayment of the balance over the new term. The advantage to Brendan and Alice is that they will retain a family home at a reduced monthly payment.

Whether this type of arrangement will work relies on an assessment of what their income and outgoings will be, and also the scale of the negative equity and the amount of trade-down required. They will also have a mortgage that may be repaid prior to retirement, thus providing financial security in their retirement.

Following the trade-down the situation will be as follows:

	Before	After
Home value	€800,000	€350,000
Loan	€1,200,000	€750,000
Loan to value (loan/value)	150%	214%
Monthly payments (4% over 25 years)	€6,334	€3,958

This simple example may not be typical of all trade-downs, but it highlights a number of issues that can arise for the borrower:

- **Interest rate** – You and your lender will need to consider the interest rate on the new loan to ensure that the deal is not so tight that a rise in rates can upset the arrangement. Also, if you are on a tracker mortgage, you will want to retain this rate.
- **Loan to value** – The borrowers may end up with a higher loan to value on the new house. If they can comfortably make the new repayments, this may be acceptable.
- **New property** – The trade-down mortgage involves moving to a house that will probably be smaller than the one you currently live in, especially if you want to stay in the same area. This deserves some consideration. You may have to ensure that the type, style and location of the property are acceptable to you for the future. As the new mortgage may be in significant negative equity you may be unable to move again in the medium term.
- **The scale of trade-down** – This may affect Brendan and Alice's ability to repay the new mortgage. In the example above the monthly repayment is still very high at €3,958 and, while it is a simple example, it highlights the inverse relationship between the initial negative equity and the possible size of the new mortgage. The bigger the initial negative equity,

the lower the price of the new house will have to be to ensure serviceability of the new mortgage.

Your lender will be looking to achieve two things:

- The smallest new mortgage possible
- Certainty that it can be serviced

As your lender possibly prefers a house sale and no new mortgage they may view a trade-down mortgage as a compromise in line with the spirit of MARP.

As there is no debt forgiveness in this situation and the negative equity is added to the new loan, the solution may result in quite a perceived drop in accommodation of the borrower. To calculate a rough estimate of the price you can afford to pay for a new property, the following methodology may be useful:

	Amount You Can Service Based on Your Income and Outgoings	Less Negative Equity in Your Existing Property	Equals New Mortgage Amount
Example 1	€750,000	€400,000	€350,000
Example 2	€550,000	€400,000	€150,000

From the above simple example it can be seen that as the negative equity is a constant it will be your ability to service a new loan amount that will dictate the purchase value of the home you can trade down too. If Brendan and Alice can only afford a €550,000 mortgage they will have €150,000 available to buy a new home.

The trade-down mortgage may work for many people, but you should do your calculations.

The trade-down mortgage is likely to be more effective for high-valued homes where a significant reduction in the loan can be achieved while leaving sufficient leeway on the new

loan to purchase an acceptable new house. It may also suit
properties that have low negative equity and where it is the
size of the mortgage that is the problem.

You need to consider all options and in particular decide
whether having a home that is not your preferred choice,
together with continued negative equity, is better than doing
a different deal with your lender.

Case Study (Continued): Alternative Proposals

Brendan and Alice have some alternative proposals to make
to their lender:

Selling the House

- They sell the house for €800,000.
- They agree to a monthly payment of €1,000 for fifteen
  years.
- They rent at €2,000 per month and improve their monthly
  cash flow.
- The bank receives €800,000 now rather than €450,000
  under the trade-down.
- There is no need to extend the €350,000 mortgage.
- The lender receives a further €180,000 over fifteen years.
  Discounting this amount at 4 per cent, it equates to a
  present value of €135,000, giving the lender a total present
  value of €935,000 against a loan of €1,200,000, or a 78 per
  cent recovery of their loan.

Debt Forgiveness

- Brendan and Alice agree to the trade-down but negotiate
  a reward, which could be an element of debt forgiveness,
  leading to a more expensive house and the same mortgage
  level.
- Alternatively, the reward could be a concessionary interest rate or nil rate on part of the loan in return for full
  capital repayment.

The above example is provided to continue to prompt you to look at all options and to reinforce the point that debt forgiveness or interest concessions have to be negotiated. There are many small negotiated adjustments that can be sought at this stage in the mortgage arrears process that may make a deal workable. The sale of the house may also be a better option if you can achieve significant debt forgiveness in return. If the right incentives are not forthcoming it may be best to seek advice on the insolvency route.

Split Mortgage

The idea behind the split mortgage concept is to split or divide the distressed mortgage into two mortgages, one repayable and the other warehoused.

1. **The affordable mortgage** – This portion of the mortgage will continue to be paid down over the earning life of the mortgage holder.
2. **The warehoused mortgage** – This portion of the mortgage is parked or set to one side for the present, but may continue to have interest charged to it.

Case Study: Split Mortgage

Chris and Helen live in a three-bedroom house in a suburb of the city. The house is valued at €300,000. However, they have a mortgage on the property of €500,000.

In addition, due to financial circumstances, they are unable to service the mortgage repayments on the €500,000 loan. Their financial adviser is assessing whether a split mortgage will work.

They are currently managing to pay interest only at 4 per cent with 25 years to run. The monthly repayments are €1,700. Based on this level of repayment ability it is considered that a mortgage of €320,000 is sustainable over 25 years at 4 per cent.

Using a split mortgage Chris and Helen would be in the following position:

- They would have an affordable mortgage of €320,000 over 25 years at a current rate of 4 per cent and monthly repayments of €1,690.
- They would have a warehoused mortgage of €180,000, which will attract monthly interest of 4 per cent.
- Assuming no reduction is made in the next 25 years, the warehoused mortgage would accumulate to approximately €488,000.
- Should their lender agree to a zero interest rate on the warehoused mortgage and they make no reductions to the warehoused loan, they will still owe the €180,000 in 25 years.

This is what their position looks like in figures:

Mortgage Split	Affordable Portion	Warehoused Portion
320/180	€320,000	€180,000
Interest rate*	4%	4%
Monthly payment	€1,690	Interest added to loan
Fast Forward 25 Years:		
Loan outstanding amount	Nil	€488,500
House value €300k (assume 2% per year)**		€492,000
Net equity in house		€3,500

*Assume constant interest for illustrative purposes.
**Assume average annual growth of 2%.

The above example is merely to illustrate the principle of a split mortgage. It is assumed that Chris and Helen will improve their earnings at some point and begin to pay down the warehouse mortgage. The extent to which they do that will dictate whether they have any equity left after 25 years, which will possibly be their retirement date. If they negotiate an interest-free warehoused loan of €180,000 they should have equity in their house but may still have a substantial loan at retirement age. Will this be acceptable and when will it be repaid?

Case Study (Continued): Counter Proposal

Chris and Helen are concerned about the following:

- Their ability to make a significant reduction in the warehoused loan is in doubt.
- They will have a constant assessment of their financial position with an emphasis to contribute more, possibly for the next 25 years.
- When the affordable loan is repaid they will be 65, with reduced retirement earnings and a significant mortgage.

Chris and Helen make a counter-proposal to their lender:

- They enter the split mortgage arrangement on revised terms.
- The warehoused loan bears no interest and stays at €180,000.
- In addition to servicing their affordable mortgage, they make payments to their lender based on 30 per cent of their increased disposable income.
- At age 65 they contribute 15 per cent of their disposable income as rent in return for a life interest in the property.
- The property is sold on the death of the last survivor to the loan.
- The lender is repaid the €180,000 warehoused loan plus 50 per cent of the remaining equity in the property.

This example illustrates that there are many variations on the deal that can be achieved. You, your lender and your adviser may have to be innovative in coming up with a solution that is acceptable to everyone. However, the deal has to have a number of critical elements for you:

- You need a deal that gives piece of mind and certainty about the future.
- You need to be able to afford it and have a decent living standard.
- You need to be able to plan and achieve a good retirement without financial worry.

Ad hoc, 'play it by ear' and reviewable yearly deals approaches will provide none of the above and should be considered carefully before you agree to them.

Below we will briefly look at some of the key issues around split mortgages.

How will I repay the warehoused mortgage?

The outstanding balance on the warehoused mortgage can be repaid from a number of sources:

- Selling the property to repay the loan – This may not be an option if there is insufficient equity to purchase a new property.
- Trading down to a smaller property – Again, this will depend on the equity value in the house.
- Releasing other assets, or a pension lump sum – Some people may be awaiting an inheritance or the receipt of a lump sum on retirement, and this can be used to repay the warehoused mortgage.
- Agree a life interest in the property – This can be useful if you are at or near retirement and cannot afford the mortgage. Rather than force a sale, your lender may agree a life

interest for you in return for a smooth transition to the sale of the property on your death. You may have to make an interest payment in the meantime.

Everyone's case is different and depending on the amount of the warehoused mortgage, the interest rate and the proposal for income growth in the future, a split mortgage can work for some people. You need to be realistic about the future as you do not want to be deeper in debt when you come to retirement. It may be best to agree such things as a life interest up front rather than hope to achieve this when you are 65. You may be tempted to accept a deal and hope for the best, but this may not be a good idea.

However, while some of the options suggested above may seem crazy or unworkable, you should try to get an incentive or reward for signing up. This will not be offered to you automatically, and if you feel awkward looking for it, it may be best to appoint a professional adviser to help you.

What is life interest?

Your solicitor can explain this and the ramifications for you and your dependants. In simple terms it is a legal arrangement whereby your lender owns the house but allows you and your spouse/partner to live in it until you both die. They will require the agreement to give them a clean sale of the house at that point.

Mortgage to Rent

The mortgage-to-rent scheme is a government initiative to help homeowners who meet certain eligibility criteria, are at risk of losing their homes and who have been involved in MARP with their lender.

The scheme is specifically targeted at low-income families whose mortgage situation is unsustainable with no prospect of change. Under the scheme the family remain in the home, paying rent, while ownership is transferred to an approved housing body.

How do you qualify?

The scheme has been developed for households that:

- Have had their mortgage deemed unsustainable under MARP
- Agree to the voluntary repossession of their home
- Do not have significant positive equity
- Are eligible for social housing

Other criteria include:

- Maximum household net income must not exceed €25,000 to €35,000 per annum (depending on regional area).
- Maximum value of the property is €220,000 in the Dublin region and €180,000 in other parts of the country.
- Borrowers must not own any other property or have assets worth more than €20,000.
- The property must fit the owners' needs (be neither over- nor under-accommodated).

What does the process involve?

- You have to surrender the house.
- The house is purchased by an approved housing body at market rate.
- The purchase is funded by a loan from the original mortgage lender (70–75 per cent) and a loan from the exchequer (25–30 per cent).
- You and your family become tenants of the approved housing body, paying a rent based on your current income and ability to pay.

Will I achieve debt forgiveness?

Perhaps, to an extent. Under this process, if there is residual debt, this is a matter between you and your lender. It is suggested that if the situation is unresolved, PIAs may in some cases come into play. So there is no automatic debt forgiveness: if you want to achieve this it must be negotiated.

Case Study

Patrick and Rosemary qualified under the mortgage-to-rent scheme, and they now hope to negotiate a deal with their lender.

The house is worth €200,000 on the open market, but Patrick and Rosemary owe €300,000.

The proposal is structured as follows:

Outstanding loan	€300,000
Purchase price to the housing association	€200,000
Funded By:	
1 Bank	€150,000
2 Exchequer	€50,000
Residual bank debt	€100,000

The residual debt of €100,000 is the responsibility of Patrick and Rosemary. What are their options?

- Will the lender write this debt off?
- Will the lender accept a monthly payment?
- If they raised a percentage of the amount, say €30,000, will the lender accept this as settlement?
- Should Patrick and Rosemary seek to resolve this issue using the personal insolvency legislation?

The outcome is unclear, and Patrick and Rosemary may need to clarify these queries before entering the deal. It is likely that the lender will also require them to be resolved prior to selling the property.

With an unsustainable mortgage and low income it would seem that an element of debt forgiveness is likely in many instances, but how much is up for negotiation.

SUMMARY

As well as the initial short-term loan modifications such as interest-only periods, lenders have introduced three longer-term solutions which they will apply to customers on a case-by-case basis.

The trade-down mortgage and the split mortgage may not seem immediately attractive, do not discount them too quickly. If you and your lender are prepared to be innovative there is a basis for a deal in many of these solutions. With an element of interest and debt forgiveness they could work.

Remember to stay focused on what any deal needs to achieve for you. Think about the following (there may be further considerations):

- You need a deal that gives piece of mind and certainty about the future.
- You need to be able to afford it and have a decent living standard.
- You need to be able to plan and achieve a good retirement without financial worry.

MARS represents a watershed in the negotiation process because if you proceed to the next level solutions – insolvency or bankruptcy – direct dialogue between you and your lender finishes and professional and legal charges start to rack up. So both sides need to consider carefully their options in the event that they cannot make MARS work.

Key Points in this Chapter

1. Longer-term solutions have been added to the mix of loan modification options:
   i. Trade-down mortgage
   ii. Split mortgage
   iii. Mortgage to rent
2. Debt forgiveness does not feature as an automatic result of these solutions.
3. The emphasis is to remain in your house and warehouse a portion of debt.
4. The trade-down mortgage involves moving to a lower-valued house and taking your negative equity in your current house with you.
5. The split mortgage involves parking or warehousing a portion of your debt, which may continue to accrue interest.
6. Mortgage to rent involves surrendering your house and renting it back.
7. All these approaches focus on what is termed an 'affordability gain', which basically means that the objective is to match your monthly repayments to your income and leave sufficient income to have a reasonable living standard.
8. The split mortgage requires particular attention as it involves annual reviews of your income with an emphasis on increasing payments from increases in disposable income. Also, there is no guarantee that you will not be in negative equity or close to it when you retire. You need to work the figures carefully on this one.
9. Everybody's case is different, and I can only give you food for thought. Some people may be very pleased with these solutions, but do the maths.
10. We have looked at MARP and MARS, but there are more options and these do place debt forgiveness firmly on the agenda.

11

The Arrears Process for Buy-to-Let Mortgages

Property investment has always been about a herd
mentality – one bank lends, so they all lend. One stops,
they all stop. It's an extremist environment, but it doesn't
mean either one is right or wrong.
James Caan, British entrepreneur and judge on BBC's
Dragons' Den

Up to now we have focused on the principal private residence, basically your home, and the solution available to
those in financial difficulty. Keeping people in their homes is
now seen as a priority, and there is good support in this area.

However, the same processes do not directly apply to
investment property mortgages. In fact, lenders have been
criticised for not taking a more robust approach to investment mortgages or what are commonly called buy-to-let
mortgages. Lenders' slowness to respond can in many cases
be attributed to the fact that it is difficult to get agreement
from borrowers to sell a property. Buy-to-let investors may
prefer to wait it out, but, in any case, they will be reluctant to
sell the property unless they know how the lender will treat
any residual debt should the property be in negative equity.
Any discussion where the lender proposes that the property
be sold first and the residual debt looked at later is unlikely
to be received warmly by a borrower. As stated, borrowers
may favour holding on to the property in the hope of better

times to come, particularly if they can in the meantime service the interest on the loan from rent or personal income.

Case Study: Buy-to-Let Mortgage

Seán has an investment property, which he purchased at the height of the boom thinking it would provide an additional financial boost in his retirement.

He released some equity from his home to support the purchase, which cost €500,000, and he now has a buy-to-let mortgage of €400,000 over 25 years at 4 per cent, with monthly capital and interest payments of €2,100.

The property is now worth €250,000, having experienced a 50 per cent fall in value. Due to a fall in income and rental levels, Seán is now unable to make the payments on the investment property.

Possible solutions from the lender include the following:

- Seán sells the family home, which still has equity, and moves into the investment property.
- Seán sells the investment property and repays the residual debt of €150,000 over the remaining life of the mortgage.
- Seán sells the property and adds the residual debt to the family home and repays the total debt over the remaining term of the loan.
- Seán may have a pension lump sum or an inheritance at a later date, which could be used to reduce the loan amount.

Possible solutions from Seán include the following:

- He would agree to one of the lender's solutions if this is workable.
- He could try to negotiate an incentive or reward for working with the lender, such as a concessionary interest rate or an element of debt forgiveness.
- He could seek to pay interest only at €1,300 and hope the property will increase in value over time.

> • He could consult a professional adviser or insolvency practitioner to explore all solutions, or have them deal with the lender to achieve an acceptable solution.
>
> Seán is aged 53 and will be 78 when the loan is due to mature.

Every individual's case is different. Some people may have one investment property; others may have several. As with the initial discussion on the family home under MARP, the initial solutions around investment properties will try to avoid debt forgiveness.

The Residual Debt Dilemma

As you will have observed from Seán's case above, much of the difficulty on both sides revolves around the residual debt. Many investors in investment properties may now regret the move and would welcome an exit. However, it is the terms of the exit that may cause the delay.

If a property is in negative equity there will be residual debt on sale. In Seán's case above, if he sells the property for the current market value of €250,000 he will still owe €150,000 to his lender, as the loan is for €400,000. It is important to remember that your liability to your lender is the *amount of your loan* rather than the value of the property.

As this is personal debt, any element of the loan not repaid after the property is sold remains with you unless your lender forgives the debt. Your lender can also, if they choose, take action to attach the residual debt to other property assets, such as your house. So seeking to establish and agree how the residual debt will be dealt with makes sense before you sell the property voluntarily.

I say 'voluntarily' because, while your lender will discuss the sale of the property with you, if negotiations break down they have more options because the property is not the family home, and they can proceed to a forced sale of the property.

If you are in difficulties on your investment there are a number of factors you need to consider in preparation for your meetings with your lender, as follows:

- Do you have equity in your family home?
- Is your spouse or partner a co-borrower on the investment property?
- Is using the new insolvency legislation or bankruptcy an option you will consider?
- Is the property servicing interest?
- Is your lender willing to provide debt forgiveness for a co-operative sale?
- What is your ability to bear residual debt? How much can you bear?

The Investment Mortgage Arrears Process

There is no specific code for buy-to-let mortgage arrears like the one that has been put in place for private residences. However, your lender is required under the Consumer Protection Code 2012 to put in place a procedure to deal with handling arrears. The Code states:

> A regulated entity must have in place written procedures for the handling of Arrears.
>
> *Consumer Protection Code 2012*
> *(Chapter 8.1)*

This procedure will more than likely follow the same five-step process outlined earlier in this book:

- **Step 1: Communication** – The Consumer Protection Code provides direction to lenders in this regard, which must be followed.

- **Step 2: Financial information** – Your lender will require financial information, which will form the basis of your discussion regarding a modification to your mortgage payment.
- **Step 3: Assessment** – Your lender will assess your financial position and consider alternative repayment arrangements.
- **Step 4: Resolution** – Your lender proposes a solution based on their assessment of your financial position.
- **Step 5: Appeal** – You have a right of appeal.

The process will be similar to the mortgage arrears process for principal private residences. Whereas the mortgage arrears process for family homes has a clear emphasis on you being left with the home, a deal on whether to retain or sell a buy-to-let property will have to be negotiated.

It is important that you analyse your situation afresh, including whether retention of the property is what you want. Your lender's desire to reduce their property book may provide an opportunity for you to exit a poor property investment. Also, put any proposal you have in writing to your lender: under the Consumer Protection Code 2012 if they reject your proposal they must formally write to you to explain why. If you decide that insolvency or bankruptcy is the only option, having a well-documented interaction with your lender may help. The Code states:

> Where arrears arise on an account and where a personal consumer makes an offer of a revised repayment arrangement that is rejected by the regulated entity, the regulated entity must formally document its reasons for rejecting the offer and communicate these to the personal consumer, on paper or on another durable medium.
>
> *Consumer Protection Code 2012*
> *(Chapter 8.12)*

Should You Hold Your Property or Sell It?

It may be opportune to review whether holding the investment property is the right option, particularly if your lender is suggesting that you sell when you are having difficulty making payments. To assist with this I will now discuss some of the elements of property development.

Rules of Investing in Property

Much of the thinking behind property investment is centred on the capital gain that can be achieved when the property goes up in value over the long term. Prior to the heady boom years, most investors in property understood this and recognised that to achieve capital growth you had to be willing to hold the property for the long term. Professional investors make their decision based on a number of key rules. Here are a few of these rules:

- **Research** – Investors should carry out proper research on the area and look for areas that have the potential for growth. They also tend to seek out properties that can be purchased at a good price and which, with some refurbishment, can deliver an increase in value. You need to assess whether your property is well located for growth, or whether it is in what is likely to be considered a secondary and unattractive location in the future.
- **Location** – We have all heard the saying that the three things you need to know about property are 'location, location, location'. For a high-fashion chain store this means the most expensive shopping street in a city, but for residential property it could just mean being in an area that is sought after for renting and where the risk of vacancies is minimal.
- **Cash flow** – 'Cash is king' is another familiar catchphrase, and if the property cannot provide sufficient income to pay the mortgage and costs you will end up subsidising it from

your income. The key here is whether your property is and will remain easy to let at an acceptable rent.

Unfortunately, many investors either ignored or were unaware of the basics when it came to property investment. They viewed a rise in property value as a one-way bet – and having witnessed the mania that surrounded property in the boom years this was an understandable mistake.

A Rough Guide to Valuation Methods

You may have purchased your property as new and therefore paid the price that was dictated by the seller's agent in a heated market. Or perhaps you bought a second-hand property, in which case you and your lender would have required a valuation to be completed by a professionally qualified estate agent.

Depending on whether a property is a site, a residential property or a trading business, the method of valuation will differ. For example, pubs and hotels may be valued based on profit, and average earnings used to establish a value. You may have noticed that at one point pubs were fetching very high prices and achieved values well beyond the bricks and mortar value of the building they operated in. The arrival of stricter drink-driving laws, the smoking ban and changed social habits has led to a downward revision in the value of pubs, due in many cases to a reduction in sales.

When it comes to residential properties and sites, estate agents use a number of methods. It is worth looking at some of these so you can consider the value of your property prior to meeting your lender.

Comparative Method

This method is used when there is good turnover in property sales in an area. The valuer may be knowledgeable about the going price of different types of property in an area and properties in different locations.

The difficulty with this method in a rising market is that you can pay too much for a property. This can impact on your ability to service the loan later as rental income is not related to what you paid but to market rents.

Investment Method

This method is used for commercial and residential invest-ment by professional investors who base their valuation on future income from the property. This method is easier to use for commercial properties where the tenant has a long lease at a set rent. The investor looks at the yield or, in simple terms, the interest rate earned on the cost of the property.

Case Study

Emma is thinking of purchasing a retail investment property. The asking price is €500,000, and the tenant has a twenty-year lease at €35,000 per annum. In simple terms this is equivalent to a 7 per cent yield or return.

Emma will also take into account location, the strength of the tenant, funding and legal costs, and potential growth in value in making her decision, but she will start with the yield and investment value compared to other options.

With the prospect of significant capital growth being seen as remote in the next five to ten years and maybe beyond, inves-tors are now adopting this methodology when considering residential purchases. This may result in values remaining stagnant for some years to come. Also, with bank interest rates over 4 per cent it means that yields significantly above this rate will be required to support any borrowing proposal if lenders return to the buy-to-let market.

Case Study

During the good years, Tom purchased a property for €500,000 when he was achieving a monthly rental income of €1,400, or €16,800 annually. This provided Tom with a gross yield on his property of 3.36 per cent.

Based on market commentary, Tom viewed this as an acceptable return as the rent was covering interest payments and he was expecting long-term capital appreciation.

The situation has now changed, as the rental income has fallen to €1,200 per month (€14,400 per annum) and Tom is advised that purchasers now consider a yield of 6 per cent as the minimum they will accept. How does this impact the value of Tom's property?

- On purchase: €16,800 per annum x 3.36% yield (€16,800/ 3.36 x 100) = €500,000
- Estimated value now: €14,400 x 6% yield (€14,400/6 x 100) = €240,000

The above example ignores the impact of rental vacancies and property costs to provide a clearer picture of how the changing attitude to property investment can dramatically impact on property values.

Before discussing your position with your lender it is worth making an assessment of the likely prospects for your property. Also think about whether there is a strong case for retaining the property, or whether it would be best to offload the property if an acceptable deal can be done with your lender.

Residual Method

This method is used for valuing development sites or properties where extensive redevelopment is likely. The valuation seeks to assess the value of a site as the residual amount after calculating the total sales value from the completed development less development costs and the property developer's profit.

Case Study

Séamus is considering the purchase of a site for the development of residential apartments. This site has planning permission for 40 apartments. Séamus estimates that the apartments will sell for €500,000 each, giving a gross sales value of €20,000,000. His quantity surveyor estimates that the cost of building the apartments, including construction, landscaping, fees and bank interest will amount to €12,000,000.

Séamus adds a profit margin equivalent to 15 per cent of total sales – €3,000,000.

With costs and sales margin coming to €15,000,000 Séamus now has a residual value of €5,000,000 on the site:

Sales value 40 apartments at €500,000	€20,000,000
Construction and financing costs	€12,000,000
Developer's profit	€3,000,000
Total costs	€15,000,000
Residual value or estimate bid price	€5,000,000

Séamus estimates that he can bid €5,000,000 for the site and achieve his projected return after all sales.

The site is estimated to have a value of €5,000,000.

This is a basic example, but it gives a flavour of how sites may be valued. It can also help to explain why site values fall further than house and apartment values. Here is Séamus from the above example in changed circumstances:

Case Study (Continued): Changed Circumstances

Séamus has purchased the site for €5,000,000. However, market sentiment has changed and demand for the apartments at €500,000 has fallen dramatically. Séamus has significant bank debt and is now considering reselling the site.

His estate agent advises that the price level for the apartments envisaged is now about €300,000, and his quantity surveyor estimates building costs before a builder's profit at €8,000,000, a 25 per cent reduction due to competitive quotes. The revised residual value is calculated as follows:

Sales value of 40 apartments at €300,000	€12,000,000
Construction and financing costs	€8,000,000
Developer's profit (15%)	€1,800,000
Total costs	**€9,800,000**
Residual value or estimate bid price	€2,200,000

The above analysis indicates that Séamus may only achieve €2,200,000 for the site. With poor market sentiment and low risk appetite among lenders, he may be relying on a cash buyer and have to take a lower offer price. While apartment prices fell by 40 per cent, the site value fell by 56 per cent. If the site is badly located or outside a main urban area it may only have value as agricultural land.

The Need to Reassess Your Property

The last few paragraphs were not intended to rub salt into your wounds, but rather to emphasise that you may need to reassess your property prior to the discussion with your lender. It could well be the case that, if you get the right deal, selling the property may be the best solution.

In any case, looking at the property anew using some of the criteria above together with the valuation methods will give you a clearer picture of what needs to happen for the property to give an adequate return and repay the lender.

By now you will be familiar with the comparative method of valuation and may have seen a significant fall in the value of your property and those in the immediate area. The fall in property values throughout the country is well documented.

What you may not be considering adequately are the prospects for the future value of your property, and you may be adopting a 'wait and see' approach, hoping that values will rise during the loan term. Some of the things you need to consider are:

- Is the cash flow from the property likely to be sufficient to cover all interest payments and costs, or will you have to inject some of your own funds? If so, how much over the lifetime of the loan?
- What are the prospects for an increase in rental levels – taking a conservative view?
- When will the loan mature, and what growth rates are needed to take out the loan?
- Given the new conservatism about buying property, what will be the expected yield and its impact on valuations over the life of your loan?

Let us look at some of these questions through examples.

Yield and Growth: The Twin Pillars of Property Investment

Property investment is an asset class with limited liquidity relative to other investments. It is also capital intensive, although many people during the boom period geared up on existing properties or took an equity release from their home to fund buying property. It also has a high dependency on cash flow to be successful, and negative cash flow is probably the main cause of property failure. Unsustainable negative cash flow will cause problems for you and your lender.

Historically, investors accepted a low yield or rental on property as they looked to the increased value of the property over time to boost the overall return. As long as the rental was considered sufficient to cover the interest and other costs, with some leeway, the investor was not concerned. Many property investments are funded on an interest-only basis due to this anticipation of capital growth and with the intention of the eventual sale providing a capital profit. To cover the risk in the meantime, lenders usually like to see that interest and costs are covered by a factor of at least 1.25 times to ensure that the loan is serviceable until maturity and sale of the property.

Should You Hold On?

If capital and interest payments are achievable, you may consider holding on to the property. As the property market is likely to remain subdued for the next seven to ten years, you need to consider whether you can commence capital and interest payments to reduce the debt or repay it so that you have the property at retirement.

Case Study

William has an investment property purchased at €400,000 with an investment mortgage of €350,000 on an interest-only basis currently at 4 per cent. The property is currently valued at €250,000.

William decides to bite the bullet and look to pay the loan off over the next 25 years until his retirement. The figures will work out as follows:

- Monthly repayments of €1,850 over 25 years at 4 per cent (assuming no rate change)
- Net rental income of €1,000 after costs
- Monthly cost to William from his own funds is €850

At age 70 William will own the property. His net outlay works out as follows:

Initial own funds	€50,000
Capital repayments	€350,000
Cost of credit	€200,000
Less net rent	€300,000
Net outlay	€300,000

The above result for William is based on him having spare cash to fund the shortfall in rent over the period and to make the capital repayments. It also depends on the property being well located, with limited vacancies. Also, you will notice that the rent is sufficient to cover the cost of credit over the period (being the total interest paid to the bank). This is due to the blended repayment structure with interest reducing as the capital is paid off.

If the loan remains on interest only the total interest over 25 years would be approximately €350,000, and with net rent of €300,000 over the period the property would cost €50,000 from William's own funds to maintain payments. At age 70 the picture would look like this:

Case Study (Continued)

At age 70 William will have outlaid the following:

Initial own funds	€50,000
Cost of credit	€350,000
Less net rent	€300,000
Net cost	€100,000
Loan outstanding	€350,000
Sale price required	€450,000

The property, currently valued at €250,000, will need to increase in value by 80 per cent or 2.4 per cent per year to liquidate William's loan and investment over the 25 years.

The above is a simplified exercise that does not take taxes, inflation and variable interest rates into account. If you are on a tracker mortgage the picture may look a lot better as the cost of credit is lower. But remember, as the European economy improves, tracker rates may move up again. However, it is worth doing this exercise with your adviser as it could help frame your approach to your lender.

We have looked at a situation with one property, but many people have multiple properties with varying degrees of attractiveness – some may be well located with good rental, and others less so. The key determinant of how you will fare over the long run with one or multiple properties will be rental yield, interest rates and capital growth, so it is helpful to evaluate your property holdings to be sure that holding on to them is the right decision.

What if I cannot service the debt and my lender is pushing for a sale?

This will require a negotiated solution, at least initially, which is why a fresh analysis of your property portfolio is recommended. You may wish to sell the property at a loss, in which case you will be trying to achieve a favourable result on the remaining debt. You could, after a full analysis, take the view that holding some or all of your properties is the best course of action and you will then have to convince your lender of this.

As investment properties are not the family home, your lender can move more quickly to force a sale and seek to attach any remaining debt to your home. Your lender will also be aware that a co-operative approach is likely to get the best result in terms of continued receipt of rental income and, if sold, a better price.

Possible solutions from the lender include the following:

- You sell the family home, which still has equity, and move into the investment property.
- You sell the property and repay the residual debt over the remaining life of the mortgage.
- You sell the property and add the residual debt to the family home.
- Consider whether a pension lump sum or an inheritance is likely in the future?

Possible solutions from you might include the following:

- You agree to one of the lender's solutions above if they will work for you.
- You negotiate an incentive or reward for working with the lender, e.g. a concessionary rate or an element of debt forgiveness.
- You consult a professional adviser or insolvency practitioner to explore all solutions or have them deal with the lender to achieve an acceptable solution.

Case Study

Molly has an investment property purchased at €400,000 with an investment mortgage of €350,000 on an interest-only basis currently at 4 per cent. The property is currently valued at €250,000.

After carrying out a full analysis and being negative about property values, Molly is seeking to negotiate an element of debt forgiveness in return for a sale of the property.

Her proposal to her lender is as follows:

- She sells the property for €250,000.
- The remaining debt after the sale is €100,000.

- This lender is to forgive €50,000.
- Molly will repay the €50,000 over ten years at the mortgage rate of 4 per cent.
- Molly will have payments of €500 per month, but she will have certainty about the future.
- The lender will have an underperforming asset off the balance sheet.
- An agreed approach saves on legal fees and may get a better price for the house.

Spouses, Partners and Guarantors

As with financial difficulties with the family home, you will have to consider others who may be party to the borrowing. This is important as, unlike the mortgage arrears process for the family home, which can go on for some time, the process for buy-to-let property can move more quickly. Guarantors in particular may need to clarify or agree a position with your lender. Where equity exists in the family home and your spouse or partner is not a party to the investment property borrowing, it may prove easier to negotiate a deal with your lender.

SUMMARY

Buy-to-let property mortgages are not afforded the same protection as family homes. Initially your lender will adopt a similar five-step approach to dealing with arrears. In relation to forcing a sale of the property, your lender has more options, so do not take their support for granted and stay active in the process. If your lender can see that they are receiving all the available rent, they will work with you. If you fail to lodge the rent they will move to rectify this, which is not that difficult for them to achieve.

Should you need some of the rent for living expenses, this will require negotiation. Eventually, if the loan does not cover interest, the question of sale will arise. This could be an opportunity to get out of the property, so do the numbers and look at the property afresh. The amount recovered will be much higher with a co-operative sale, but if you are not working with your lender they will not be afraid to take a loss. Any residual debt will remain with you, so make sure you keep the repayment method of this on the agenda.

Key Points in this Chapter

1. Buy-to-let mortgages are treated differently from mortgages on family homes.
2. Many interest-only, buy-to-let loans were advanced by lenders and are now in significant negative equity or may have an interest shortfall.
3. It is more likely that your lender will seek a sale of properties that cannot cover interest, unless you can cover the shortfall.
4. Your lender has more options when it comes to a forced sale of buy-to-let properties, but they will still look for a co-operative sale.
5. If a sale will result in a residual debt you need to get clarity on how this will be dealt with and put an element of debt forgiveness or a long repayment term on the agenda.
6. Resolutions such as adding the residual debt to your existing mortgage or repayment over an extended period may be suggested.
7. It is worth making an honest reassessment of why you should hold the property and what needs to happen in terms of yield, interest rates and growth rates to get you out comfortably.
8. As always, ensure that all parties to the borrowing are kept involved. If your spouse is not on the mortgage this may improve the chances of an acceptable deal.
9. Talking to an adviser early is possibly more important with buy-to-let properties as your lender will not be as inhibited in taking action.
10. Be prepared to consider your other options, such as personal insolvency.

Part IV

Personal Insolvency and Bankruptcy: New Measures to Tackle the Personal Debt Crisis

In the final part of this book I will review the new solutions enacted to deal with mortgage arrears and personal debt. This refers to the new legislation on personal insolvency and the amendments to the bankruptcy laws.

Should you be unable to reach an acceptable solution to your problem with MARP and MARS, you may need to look at these other options.

This part of the book will give you an insight into what personal insolvency and bankruptcy entail and show you that looking at all options with your financial adviser, even before making any decisions with your lender, is worth consideration.

12

Is Personal Insolvency for You?

Today knowledge has power. It controls access to
opportunity and advancement.

Peter F. Drucker, US author, educator and
management consultant

Why Consider Insolvency?

Like MARP, the new insolvency legislation is designed to provide relief to those in serious financial difficulties while ensuring that the gates are not open for wide-scale abuse. This is a difficult balancing act, and a number of checks and balances are placed within the system to achieve the desired end. The process could prove long and arduous with no guarantee of getting your intended result. Many commentators see the lenders' position as being too strong to allow for effective agreement.

However, the fact is that the taxpayer has funded some lenders to allow them to deal with the problem of mortgage difficulties, and you can be sure that many people will achieve debt forgiveness as a result. The course may be long and arduous and require much financial stamina, but those who survive it should achieve a positive result.

Lenders have been writing off debts since banking began, and right now it is just the size of the personal debt problem that is proving overwhelming. However, your lender wants to be rid of this problem and will eventually take steps to resolve it. Those who are informed and proactive in managing their problem will achieve most.

Look at it this way. If you were sure you could save €50,000 on your debt, how many hours would you be prepared to spend getting yourself informed on how you might achieve that? For a person earning €15 per hour this is the equivalent of 3,300 hours or 83 weeks' work. When you take into account that a mortgage is paid out of after-tax income the argument for making an informed assessment of your financial position is clear.

Remember, the principle behind all the codes and legislation is that those who cannot pay should be given assistance. While the nature and amount of that assistance requires negotiation you owe it to yourself and your dependants to assess whether you are a deserving case.

Another principle of the codes and legislation is keeping people in their homes. This could be a double-edged sword. If you get fixated on having to stay in your house it can weaken your negotiating position as you have set a precondition which the lender can exploit.

Personal Debt Is Personal: It Stays with You

Personal debt is, as the term implies, personal to you, which makes it harder to avoid. In company law a company is considered a separate entity from the shareholders who own it. A company with financial difficulties can enter a legal process called examinership and, if successful, may receive relief from its creditors, write off debts and renegotiate leases on properties.

All this is achieved through the courts and under the stewardship of a qualified accountant. The accountant, after talking to various creditors, presents a proposal to the court and in many cases achieves the objective of allowing the company to continue in business. Creditors take their losses, landlords may reduce their rents and all can then decide whether they will continue to do business with each other. Many companies do not get to examinership as they are not viable – they simply liquidate. Again, there are set court procedures here, and creditors who are owed money often lose out.

As mentioned, companies are seen as separate entities in law and, effectively, are treated like another person. This means that company debts belong to the company and not the shareholders or directors of the company. They are separate, and any losses inflicted on creditors remain the responsibility of the company, unless the debts of the company have been guaranteed personally by the shareholders or directors. This is the concept of limited liability, which goes with operating a business through a company structure rather than in a person's name.

Personal loans have no such protection, as the limited liability that applies to companies and, in the main, a person is fully responsible for any debt. This means that your creditors can pursue you for the debt and seek to recover it from what assets you own. In the case of a mortgage, for example, your liability is the loan amount, not the value of the property. If you sell the property and recover less than the outstanding loan, you still owe the balance on that loan.

Case Study

Consider the following scenarios:

- Stephen and Sarah owe €200,000 to the bank on a property valued at €150,000. They sell the property for €150,000. They must now repay the lender the remaining balance on the loan of €50,000. Stephen and Sarah must negotiate with the lender as to how the remaining balance of €50,000 is paid.

> • Stephen and Sarah Ltd, a limited liability company, owes €200,000 to the lender on a property valued at €150,000. The company sells the property for €150,000. Stephen and Sarah have no direct liability for the €50,000 unless they have guaranteed the company debt.

This is a simple illustration of the difference between personal debt and the law that currently exists for limited liability companies. It provides the backdrop for the new legislation which, in a sense, is seeking to achieve a similar structure whereby individuals in difficulty with personal debt have a process by which it can be resolved.

How Is Personal Debt To Be Resolved?

While the legal structure for resolving company debt exists and is working satisfactorily, the proposal to deal with personal debt revolves around three processes. We have already discussed the first of these processes, MARP, and if you have failed to achieve a satisfactory result using this process it may be time to consider insolvency or bankruptcy as an option.

We will set the context and provide an overview of the insolvency legislation in this chapter and go into it in more detail in Chapter 13 on unsecured debt and Chapter 14 on secured debt (including mortgages). Bankruptcy will be covered in Chapter 15.

Follow the Flow

The legislation implies that in order to resolve their debt difficulty, individuals will go through the processes in order, starting with MARP. You can enter the personal insolvency process after an unsuccessful interaction with your lender for a period of six months. It is possible to go straight to bankruptcy if a home owner feels that this is most appropriate. However, the amendments to the bankruptcy legislation seem to suggest that, particularly in relation to mortgage debt, it will be used as a last resort after exhausting the other processes.

It does make sense to try to go through the earlier processes first and, in doing so, build both your experience and your case for the outcome you feel is fair and acceptable to all. The reason for this is that if you take the final step towards bankruptcy you will want to show that you have made a genuine attempt to resolve the problem. Under the new legislation the court dealing with bankruptcy can, if it sees fit, stall proceedings and refer the parties back to seek a resolution under the personal insolvency legislation.

We now have a process in place to handle personal debt problems, and this should lead to debt forgiveness. However, it will be hard fought, and only those who can prove insolvency and convince their lenders that the solution they propose is the best course of action will be successful – and possibly only after staying the full course.

The message consistently remains that you must do your financial homework, present a fair and reasonable case, record all interactions and stay engaged in the process.

The Size of the Problem Is Immense

The change in approach required to allow the new insolvency legislation to work is dramatic. While many people agree that debt forgiveness on personal debt is necessary to reinvigorate the economy, increase spending and release people from financial slavery, the fact is that it is something we are not used to on such a major scale.

As we have seen from the solutions put forward in Parts II and III of this book, the emphasis is on debt servicing while you remain in your house, but with no debt forgiveness. In essence, your lender may be offering relief on a daily cash management basis through modified loan payments, which means more money in your pocket but no debt reduction. This may be all you need. Alternatively, you could be just putting off the inevitable and trying to ignore what is a real financial problem.

Your lender may be hoping that things will improve for you. Either your economic circumstances will change and allow you to recommence paying down the loan over its life, or a rising property market will reduce your negative equity. Your lender may be looking to your future earning capacity and ultimately to the sale value of the property at a future date. Your individual problem is multiplied across your lender's personal loan book for all customers.

Case Study

Ann is a civil servant. She is in her early 30s and has ten years' service. She purchased a two-bed apartment in a city centre location with a friend in 2004 and later purchased the friend's share at the height of the boom. The property is valued at €175,000 but the bank loan is €350,000.

Ann also has significant personal debt taken out for personal goods and study courses purchased in better times.

She is feeling the impact of the government salary and pension adjustments. She rents a room to help subsidise payments. However, Ann is unable to service the mortgage repayments.

Her lender's view of her situation is as follows:

- They will review Ann's budgets and see what is payable. They will look for interest plus some capital.
- Ann is studying and may achieve promotion and salary increases in the future.
- Property may improve in value over the years.
- Overview of strategy: support the borrower until better times and review her case every six months.

Ann's view is as follows:

- She is happy to get the lender's support and will persist with the situation.
- She is unable to see an alternative or any ability to move out of the property.
- She hopes to move to a new property and rent out her apartment.

Things to consider:

- Can Ann prove insolvency and look for some debt forgiveness?
- Can she consider bankruptcy and start again?
- What would be the impact of either option on her employment?
- Should she sell the property and cut a deal on the residual debt?

This fictitious case will be fairly typical of many people's approach when provided with an initial solution by their lender. As stated many times in this book, your lender is unlikely to go directly to a solution that involves debt forgiveness and will more than likely only go there in extreme cases. While it is possible to achieve debt forgiveness using MARP, it is unlikely unless you press your case strongly and your lender sees no better course of action. Many people will not explore the possibility of insolvency or do not consider themselves to be insolvent. The reason for this is that they look at their lifetime earnings in assessing their solvency, thinking that they will eventually work their way out of debt.

We will shortly show you that there are many rules that you and your insolvency practitioner must follow to achieve a PIA, and advice is needed on your individual case. However, a key element of the legislation is that you only need to be certified as being insolvent by a personal insolvency practitioner to be eligible to enter a PIA. This is covered in the legislation as follows:

> ... having considered the Prescribed Financial Statement completed by the debtor [*you*] ... [*and considered some other matters in the legislation*] ... it is his or her opinion [*the opinion of your personal insolvency practitioner*] there is no likelihood of the debtor [*you*] becoming solvent within the period of **5 years** commencing on the date of making of the declaration.
>
> *Paraphrased from the Personal Insolvency Act 2012*

Two of the key requirements when looking for an alternative solution are:

- Are you insolvent right now?
- Are you likely to be insolvent in the next five years?

It is not a requirement that you remain insolvent for the rest of your life. We posed the following question earlier, but it is worth repeating:

How do I prove personal insolvency?

You will have to enlist the assistance of a personal insolvency practitioner, who will help you determine this and, more important, assess your eligibility for a PIA.

However, the following working definition gives the basic principle and test of personal insolvency:

> A person is insolvent if they have insufficient assets to pay their debts and financial liabilities. The Insolvency Act states that 'insolvent' in relation to a debtor shall be construed as meaning that the debtor is unable to pay his or her debts in full as they fall due.

As mentioned in Chapter 2, there are two primary tests for determining insolvency:

1. **The cash flow test** – An individual is regarded as insolvent if they are unable to pay debts as they fall due.
2. **The balance sheet test** – An individual is insolvent if total liabilities outweigh the value of assets.

As pointed out in Chapter 2 the definition of insolvency in the Act seems to confine insolvency to the cash flow test. So it may be worth talking to an insolvency practitioner, then making an assessment of your financial position for the next five years, and checking out whether entering the insolvency process will positively or negatively impact on your position. Then review your options.

Case Study

Jonathan is an entrepreneur builder who developed high-quality properties during the boom years. As business grew he purchased more development sites to accommodate future business expansion.

He is now sitting on loans of €10,000,000 with property assets of €3,000,000. His family home is valued at €1,000,000 with no mortgage, but he is personally liable for the €10,000,000 of debt. He is now looking at his options:

1. The bank would like to see the sites sold and also want him to move to a smaller house and release some of the equity in the €1,000,000 home to them.
2. As his secured debt is over €3,000,000 he cannot choose personal insolvency, which only applies on borrowings of up to €3,000,000 of secured debt.
3. He could take the bankruptcy route, which would require the sale of all assets, including the family home, and be free of all his debt in three years. If his wife is not liable

---

> on any of the debt and only Jonathan is made bankrupt she can claim her portion of the house proceeds.
>
> Jonathan is confident that he can earn some income over the three years and get back into building when things improve.
> Maybe he should contact an insolvency practitioner and look at his options.

Jonathan has a very large debt burden, which he may feel he is unlikely to be in a position to repay. However, he is also self-employed, has skills with which he can generate an income in the future, and is not dependent on salaried employment for a living. Some of these elements may make it easier for people like Jonathan to take the bankruptcy route, which has traditionally been associated with a 'fresh start' for business people.

However, it is worth emphasising that the personal insolvency legislation seems to accommodate the concept of debt forgiveness while people remain in their current employment and is available to those who can prove they are eligible. Bankruptcy also seems to assume that a person will have an income during the process. Apart from trades or professions that exclude bankrupt persons from practising their trade or profession, the bankruptcy laws would seem to allow most salaried people to remain in their jobs.

Do I get to stay in my house?

All processes, except bankruptcy, have an emphasis on you being able to remain in your family home, so it is more than likely that you will be able to do so. Levels 1 and 2, which are covered by the Code of Conduct on Mortgage Arrears, are strongly focused on allowing you to remain in your home and, as I have pointed out, the solutions they offer involve deferring debt and interest payments rather than debt forgiveness. In other words, you stay in your home and keep the same level of debt.

If you are heavily in debt or insolvent you may need to get debt forgiveness on the agenda at Levels 1 and 2 or consider options that involve the sale of your home.

Even at Level 3 the personal insolvency legislation proposes that any plan prepared by your personal insolvency practitioner should aim at not requiring you to sell your home, subject to certain tests, which include:

- The cost of remaining in the home (including rent, mortgage loan repayments, insurance, management fees, taxes, etc.)
- Your income and other financial circumstances as disclosed in your financial statement
- Your reasonable living and accommodation needs
- The cost of staying in the house versus alternative accommodation

The point here is that while it is not certain that you will be able to stay in your home under a PIA, the legislation provides for considering and analysing this outcome. It may come down to the appropriateness of the house to family size and income, and the solution may involve having a family home, but not the one you are currently living in – in other words, trading down to a smaller house.

Will I have enough to live on?

Here again the personal insolvency legislation provides assistance. It specifies that any PIA should not require you to make payments to your lenders when you do not have sufficient income to maintain a reasonable standard of living for you and your dependants. The Personal Insolvency Act 2012 states:

A personal insolvency agreement should not contain any terms which would require the debtor to make payments of such an amount that the debtor would not have sufficient income to maintain a reasonable standard of living for the debtor and his/her dependants.

However, it will be up to the Insolvency Service to provide guidance on what is a reasonable standard of living.

As we have pointed out, at Levels 1 and 2 the mortgage arrears process will require you to complete a standard financial statement outlining your assets, liabilities, income and outgoings. Your lender will seek to restrict outgoings so that you can at least pay interest and perhaps some capital. Accordingly, there is no set formula. It may well be the case that when guidance is provided on what a reasonable standard of living is, it will be adopted across the financial sector.

However, it is quite possible that setting a reasonable standard of living will be problematic. Different social groups have different expectations of living standards. They also have different expectations of lifestyle and accommodation. Will a reasonable standard of living be set in relation to your past income or living standards, or will it be a case of 'one size fits all'?

SUMMARY

We now have legislation that provides a genuine structure for individuals to deal with their personal debt problems. It is the responsibility of each person experiencing difficulties with their financial position to inform themselves of the processes that are now in place to help. The mortgage arrears process MARP is a good start for those whose problems relate to their family home, and this process will also initially help buy-to-let investors.

Many people are financially insolvent at present, to a greater or lesser extent, and the new legislation is designed to address this fact. If you cannot see an acceptable way out of your financial difficulties, and your lenders are not coming up with a solution that you feel is right, there is no harm in talking to a personal insolvency practitioner to establish your other options.

Key Points in this Chapter

1. We now have a process that puts debt forgiveness on the agenda under the personal insolvency legislation.

2. To engage in this process you will need to enlist the assistance of a personal insolvency practitioner.

3. Your personal insolvency practitioner will first assess whether you are eligible under the legislation. If you are eligible, you can start the process.

4. Your personal insolvency practitioner will get you initial protection from your lender and other creditors and will start a discussion with them on possible solutions.

5. Your personal insolvency practitioner is the only person who can interact with your lender and other creditors. In effect, they represent you.

6. The objective of your personal insolvency practitioner is to reach a PIA with your lender and other creditors, under which you will make certain payments over the following six or seven years, with a release from certain debts thereafter.

7. As your lender and other creditors must vote on the arrangement, and this is a majority vote, some commentators feel the lenders may have too strong a hand.

8. Any result will rely on your personal insolvency practitioner constructing a deal that you can live with, but is seen by your lenders and other creditors as the best option for them.

9. The insolvency legislation aims to enable you to stay in your house and have a reasonable standard of living.

10. Assessing your ability to avail of the insolvency process makes sense within your overall plan for resolving your debt problems. Whether you take this step is up to you.

13

Personal Insolvency: Unsecured Debt

Place a higher priority on discovering what a win looks like for the other person.
Harvey Robbins, US entrepreneur and leadership coach

This chapter takes a broad look at personal insolvency to give you a sense of what it entails and then discusses which of the three processes outlined in the legislation will be of use to you. The processes that deal with unsecured debt will be looked at in this chapter, and the process more relevant to mortgage holders will be dealt with in Chapter 14.

Insolvency vs Bankruptcy

There are many avenues to follow before you choose either personal insolvency or bankruptcy as the way to deal with your problem. However, it is worth having some knowledge of what insolvency and bankruptcy entail from the beginning of your negotiation with your lender. This is the only way you can adequately assess any new arrangement that is proposed and whether, if it comes to it, you are prepared to take either of these options.

Your negotiations will be improved if you are armed with the following:

- An assessment by a personal insolvency practitioner as to your eligibility for insolvency. If you are not eligible, this option is ruled out. If you are eligible, your insolvency practitioner may be able to give you an indication of what is achievable in insolvency.
- The knowledge of the ramifications of bankruptcy for you and your dependants and whether this is an option in your particular case. Will you recover quickly financially? Are all the stakeholders in your life happy with this route?

It should not be assumed that you will do better with insolvency or bankruptcy, but exploring these options provides you with a means of comparing different offers or options available to you. It will also help you focus on what you want to achieve.

Many commentators focus solely on debt forgiveness, but your preferred goal may be a good lifestyle for you and your dependants. Achieving debt forgiveness and having to live in financial austerity for the next 25 years may not be your goal. Achieving a lower interest rate, a deferment of debt or some other arrangement may be preferable to debt forgiveness if you can live well enough to allow you to get back on your feet.

Case Study

Frank and Susan have been offered a deal by their lender but are conflicted and confused.

The deal their lender has offered just does not sit right with them. They feel that signing the deal commits them to many years of hardship and they cannot see how they would be better off in the end. They are asking a number of questions:

- Is it worth it for the house?
- Is their lender giving them an acceptable deal?
- Though they would prefer not to, is it time to walk away from the negotiation? But to where?

> They have heard that personal insolvency can result in them having an acceptable debt level within six years and bankruptcy may leave them debt free within three years.
>
> Both of these sound a lot better than what's on offer now – but what are the downsides?
>
> They decide to get informed.

Media comment suggests that the new insolvency legislation is likely to be used by between six thousand and ten thousand people, after they have assessed the benefit it provides relative to the other options proposed by their lender. The remainder of those with financial difficulties will deal directly with their lender and will be focused on achieving a solution that does not involve insolvency.

This may be the case, and you may more than likely achieve an acceptable deal with your lender, but knowledge of all possible outcomes will strengthen your hand.

Most lenders have a number of longer-term solutions that they are willing to consider, but they emphasise debt deferral over debt forgiveness. The arrangements on offer are one of the following:

- **Trade-down mortgage** – This option is designed for those in mortgage difficulties with high-value or larger properties. The idea is that they trade down to a lower-value house and carry the negative equity with them.
- **Split mortgage** – The distressed mortgage is split into two mortgages, one repayable and the other warehoused:
  - The *affordable mortgage* will continue to be paid down over the earning life of the mortgage holder.
  - The *warehoused mortgage* is parked or set to one side for the present, but may or may not continue to have interest charged to it.
- **Mortgage to rent** – This is a government initiative to help homeowners who meet certain eligibility criteria and are at risk of losing their homes, and who have been involved in

MARP with their lender. The scheme is specifically targeted at low-income families whose mortgage situation is unsustainable with no prospect of change. Under the scheme the family remain in the home, paying rent, while ownership is transferred to an approved housing body.

These are the opening solutions, which are being tested by the lenders, and it is likely that they will be refined over the next year based on practical application. It is quite likely that some debt forgiveness, or at least interest forgiveness, will form part of the solution in many cases.

When your lender offers you one of these options, they may be willing to finance a consultation between you and a qualified professional accountant who will explain the deal to you, but will not provide a recommendation. While this will save money, it may be best to pay extra and get full advice on your best course of action. This is your decision.

Personal Insolvency: An Overview

The new insolvency legislation provides for the reform of personal insolvency laws and introduces three new non-judicial debt resolution procedures, subject to relevant conditions in each process. 'Non-judicial' means that, while the courts have a monitoring role over the process, the actual agreement will be between you and your lender. In fact you cannot engage directly with your lender in this process, so you must use the services of a professional called a personal insolvency practitioner The Insolvency Service of Ireland is also involved.

The three new processes are:

1. **Debt Relief Notice (DRN)** – This allows you to write off qualifying eligible debt up to €20,000, either by paying half of the debts or by following a three-year supervision period.

2. **Debt Settlement Arrangement (DSA)** – This allows for the agreed settlement of unsecured debt over €20,000 to one or more creditors. This can lead to a discharge from a portion of your current debt after five years, as long as you adhere to the agreed arrangement.
3. **Personal Insolvency Arrangement (PIA)** – This process, which includes secured debt up to €3,000,000, allows a debtor to pay a portion of what is due to creditors over six or seven years and then be discharged from further liability.

Achieving the solutions outlined above is not as easy as it looks – there are eligibility criteria and rules, and your lender must agree – but they are of sufficient interest for you to explore as part of your strategy to solve your financial difficulties.

In addition to the introduction of the three new insolvency processes above, the legislation introduces significant changes to the Bankruptcy Act 1988, the most significant of which is a reduction in the bankruptcy period from twelve years to three years.

As stated, the new arrangements for insolvency and bankruptcy come with conditions, so achieving a result requires analysis, patience and negotiation. A major benefit of this legislation is that it comes with rules and timelines for both you and your lender, so it cannot be ignored or drawn out.

PIAs are designed for those with a secured borrowing such as a mortgage, whether on a private residence or investment property, and we will look at these in the next chapter. First we will deal with the two other processes that cater for unsecured debt, namely DSAs and DRNs.

DSAs: The Solution for Unsecured Debt

This process allows for the agreed settlement of unsecured debt over €20,000 to one or more creditors. This can lead to a discharge from a portion of your current debt after five years, subject to adhering to the agreed arrangement.

This is the basic objective of DSAs. As we will also see with PIAs for secured debt, there are eligibility criteria, and you are also required to engage a personal insolvency practitioner to deal on your behalf with your lenders and other creditors.

Your personal insolvency practitioner will assess your eligibility for the process. The criteria include the following:

- You must be insolvent (see Chapter 12).
- You must make a full financial statement in a prescribed format. This document is sworn.
- As this is unsecured debt, there is no ceiling on the amount of debt (unlike a PIA for secured debt, which has a limit of €3,000,000).
- You must be domiciled in Ireland or ordinarily resident here or have had a place of business in the state, within one year before the date of the application for a protective certificate. As these are taxation terms your adviser can assess these, but most citizens will qualify under these definitions.
- There are some debts – termed excluded debts – that cannot be reduced as part of an insolvency arrangement, whether a PIA, DSA or DRN. These relate to, among other things, domestic payments and damages awarded by the courts. Other government debts such as taxes and rates are termed 'excludable debts' and can be included if these creditors agree. Your personal insolvency practitioner can review these with you if appropriate.
- The process lasts five years.

If your personal insolvency practitioner is satisfied that you qualify for the insolvency process they will make an application for a protective certificate to the Insolvency Service of Ireland. If the Insolvency Service is satisfied with what has been presented, it will apply to the court for a protective certificate. If issued, the certificate will give you protection from your lenders and other creditors for 70 days, and an extension of a further 40 days is achievable if progress on a solution is proven.

All of this will be managed by your personal insolvency practitioner, but it is also worth remembering the following points:

- You only get one opportunity during your lifetime to use this process.
- Any proposal put to your lenders and other creditors requires 65 per cent voting approval to be accepted.
- The process is reviewed once a year, and any improvement in your position can lead to a variation in the proposal.
- If you default on the arrangement or are in arrears for six months, the DSA is terminated and you become liable for all debt covered by the arrangement, including arrears, interest and charges.

In summary, this process may help achieve agreement on unsecured debt with your lenders and other creditors. Just like the PIAs we will discuss in the next chapter, it relies on proving eligibility, engaging a personal insolvency practitioner and striking an acceptable deal with your creditors.

If I have secured debt and unsecured debt, which process do I use?

A DSA is a separate process, so if you have significant unsecured debt over €20,000 with no upper ceiling you can deal with this to the exclusion of your secured creditors. However, you cannot get protection from your secured creditors unless you take the PIA route (see Chapter 14).

Your secured lenders may be happy not to take action unless they have some unsecured debt on which you are seeking debt forgiveness. It may depend on how interconnected your lending is and how many different lenders you have. As you must also use a personal insolvency practitioner for DRNs and DSAs, they will be able to advise you on the best course of action.

If you have a distinct and separate group of unsecured lenders you can deal with them using the DSA.

Can a DSA be used to deal with residual debt?

This is an interesting question which may not be fully answerable until the legislation is fully operational, and it may require a legal expert to figure out each case.

Case Study

Matthew has a single property which is now valued at €200,000. His outstanding mortgage is €350,000. He has lost his job and is now working freelance at a much lower salary level.

He is considering selling the property and has an offer of €210,000. He is asking himself the following questions:

- Can he insist on the lender taking the offer?
- If they refuse, can he legally provide possession of the property to the bank?
- If he sells for €210,000 and has a residual debt of €140,000, is this unsecured debt and can he use the DSA to achieve an acceptable deal?
- If the bank vetoes a DSA, is he prepared to consider bankruptcy?

Matthew needs to consult a personal insolvency practitioner to resolve some of his questions.

Another example of where residual debt is likely to arise is with one of the MARS long-term solutions discussed in Part III of this book, namely the mortgage-to-rent scheme. If the property has been purchased from the lender at market value this may leave a residual debt to be dealt with by the borrower and the lender. The suggestion is that this may have to be resolved using the personal insolvency legislation if no agreement can be reached otherwise.

What is secured and unsecured debt?

There will no doubt be much legal wrangling in the coming months as to which debt qualifies as secured debt and which qualifies as unsecured debt.

The Personal Insolvency Act 2012 (Part 1, Clause 2) states that:

> … 'security' means, in relation to a debt, any means of securing a payment of a debt and includes –
>
> (a) a mortgage, judgment mortgage, charge, lien, pledge, hypothecation or other security interest or encumbrance or collateral in or over any property (whether real or personal and including choses-in-action),
> (b) an assignment by way of security, and
> (c) an undertaking or agreement by any person (including a solicitor) to give or create a security interest in property.

This implies that secured debt is where a lender has a formal charge on some property or asset, but also seems to include undertakings to provide a charge. Much of the lending carried out during the boom years was secured by less formal structures, such as guarantees, undertakings, etc. It is important to establish which category the security you have provided falls into. It may be that the debt you felt was secured is in fact unsecured debt, or vice versa. Remember that while a DSA is unlimited as to the amount of debt that can be included, a PIA is restricted to €3,000,000 of secured debt.

Does my lender have a veto?

As with all the processes to resolve your financial difficulties, you need to provide a proposal that incentivises your creditor in a way that makes the 65 per cent majority believe is better for them than going down the bankruptcy route. The amendments to the bankruptcy laws will make creditors think carefully before taking this option, but do not take this for granted. You must also ensure that you can adhere to any deal agreed.

DRNs: The Solution for Small Unsecured Debt

This process covers small unsecured debts up to €20,000. (It is not directly relevant to mortgage holders in arrears.)

The main features are:

- The process allows for the write-off of qualifying debts up to €20,000 either by paying half of the debts or after a three-year supervision period.
- As well as qualifying debts of €20,000 or less, there are other conditions required to be eligible for this process. The key conditions are:
  - You must have net disposable income of €60 or less per month.
  - You must have assets or savings of no more than €400.
  - You must be insolvent and have no realistic prospect of being able to pay your debts within three years of the application.
- There are a number of other conditions, which can be covered by your financial intermediary.
- Qualifying debts include credit card debt, an overdraft or unsecured bank loan, and bills in respect of utility bills or rent.
- You will need to review excluded and excludable debts with your financial intermediary to see which can be negotiated

and, if applicable, which must be paid, as they are outside the DNR process.
- Secured debt can be included. However, when the DRN ceases, the secured creditors retain the right to enforce their security.

SUMMARY

The government has now put in place new legislation to deal with the personal debt crisis and allow those in most need to seek to resolve their personal financial difficulties in a formal structure. This chapter gave an overview of the processes and what is involved to help you with your decision making. It is mandatory that you enlist the services of a professional under these processes, and they will be able to assess your eligibility to enter one or more of the three processes designed to deal with personal debt.

The three new processes are:

1. **Debt Relief Notice (DRN)** – This deals with unsecured debt up to €20,000.
2. **Debt Settlement Arrangement (DSA)** – This deals with unsecured debt over €20,000.
3. **Personal Insolvency Arrangement (PIA)** – This deals with secured debt up to €3,000,000.

Each process has rules and eligibility criteria for both you and for what debt can be included. In all cases, you need a professional adviser to work for you, but for DSAs and PIAs you need a personal insolvency practitioner to engage on your behalf with your lender.

If you feel your difficulties cannot be resolved by the solution being proposed by your lender, this new legislation is worth considering. It may also be of value in your early negotiation with your lender to know whether you can opt for the personal insolvency route, so a consultation with a personal insolvency practitioner may be useful.

Key Points in this Chapter

1. We have covered two processes under the insolvency legislation which deal with unsecured debt. These are the Debt Relief Notice (DRN) for qualifying unsecured debt up to €20,000 and the Debt Settlement Arrangement (DSA) for unsecured debt over €20,000 and with no upper ceiling.

2. The key to DSAs is to ensure that you can stick to what is agreed. If you default you can become liable for all the debt again – your deal will unravel.

3. If you wish to avoid bankruptcy while at the same time achieving a deal, you may have to convince your creditors that the proposal you offer is better than what will be achieved by bankruptcy.

4. If you achieve a deal and adhere to the terms agreed you should be free of unsecured debt after five years. Secured creditors retain their rights.

5. Under a DSA there is provision for a reasonable standard of living during the five-year period.

6. It is unlikely that you will have to give up your home. However, in certain circumstances you may have to trade down.

7. You need to make an accurate assessment of your secured and unsecured debt, as some forms of security provided may be considered under the legislation to be an unsecured loan.

8. Unsecured creditors can be dealt with separately under a DSA. However, it is best to seek the opinion of your personal insolvency practitioner on this.

9. Reasonable living expenses are catered for in the process.

10. An early meeting with a personal insolvency practitioner will answer many of the questions you may have and establish whether this is a viable option.

14

Personal Insolvency: Secured Debt

We cannot change the cards we are dealt, just how we play the hand.
Randy Pausch, US university professor of computer science

This chapter will focus on the insolvency process that will be of most interest to those with mortgage arrears, whether on the family home or buy-to-let properties, i.e. the Personal Insolvency Arrangements (PIAs), which are intended to address all personal debt difficulties (subject to restrictions) rather than just the family home. The process includes all unsecured personal debt and secured debt up to €3,000,000. First, however, I am going to review the distinction between insolvency and bankruptcy.

Insolvency and Bankruptcy: What Is the Difference?

You may question why the estimated number of those availing of the insolvency legislation is as high as 10,000 when there are so few bankruptcies in Ireland – fifty to a hundred per year. The reason for this is that insolvency is not the same as bankruptcy.

Insolvency does not have the same impact on your lifestyle or restrictions on working. It may be of particular benefit to professional people and entrepreneurs as they may be able to remain working during the insolvency period and be out of the process in six or seven years with substantially reduced debt. One of the impacts of bankruptcy is that a professional person may be prohibited from practising their profession after being made bankrupt. For an entrepreneur anxious to get back to business there will be restrictions placed on them relating to their participation in any new business venture.

For those who can generate an income based on their innate or acquired skill and are not tied to a particular company, the insolvency legislation may prove useful, but you cannot just opt for insolvency and achieve it. The deal with your lenders is subject to agreement. With multiple lenders there are prescribed acceptance levels that have to be met, but, once agreed, significant debt forgiveness can be achieved.

The other major difference between insolvency and bankruptcy is that the insolvency legislation seeks to have you remain in your home, whereas bankruptcy leads to its sale. With insolvency you may also have a better chance of negotiating an acceptable standard of living for you and your family as you will be dealing with your lenders, who may trade off a better living standard for less debt forgiveness.

In bankruptcy your affairs are handled by a court-appointed official who sells all your assets and distributes the proceeds to your creditors. While you remain in bankruptcy they will allow you living expenses, which you may not find acceptable.

Are You Ready to Consider Insolvency?

Let us assume that you have done everything right so far. You have made an accurate assessment of your living expenses and full disclosure of your assets and liabilities, entered into the mortgage arrears process and now, following assessment, your lender has offered you a deal in writing. However, the deal may not be acceptable to you. Perhaps you feel that you cannot keep to the payment structure offered, or it is so restrictive that you cannot see yourself having a decent living standard for many years to come. Perhaps it involves a proposal to sell your house, either immediately or within a given timeframe. What can you do in this situation?

First, you can appeal the decision with your lender. Under the Code of Conduct on Mortgage Arrears the lender must establish an appeals board to consider any appeals made by borrowers who are not happy to proceed with a proposal put forward by the arrears support unit.

If you appeal, there will be an independent review of your position by people who have not been directly involved in your case. The key point to note is that if you cannot achieve an agreement with your lender's support unit, you can appeal the decision. It can take up to 40 days to assess your appeal. During this period your lender cannot take action to repossess your house, so you have no need to worry about that. It provides a breathing space for you to consider your options should your appeal be rejected. It will also provide time to consider whether the lender's deal is workable as presented or with some adjustments.

What About Repossession?

If you decide to appeal your lender's proposal you may start to worry, and this may lead you to agree to an unworkable deal.

The fact is, the last thing your lender wants is your home. Repossessions in Ireland are quite low as a percentage of mortgages. The same is true of bankruptcy. The mortgage arrears process is designed to keep you in your home if at all possible. Repossessions and bankruptcies are expensive and time-consuming for the lender because both involve a court-based legal process.

In addition, if the situation comes to this, your lender will fear that you will stop paying money towards your mortgage and lose interest in the property. If the lender achieves possession, they could end up with a significant legal bill and, unless the property is well maintained, a reduction in the value of the property. The process also makes it harder to achieve a good market price for the property, as purchasers may perceive it as an opportunity to get a bargain property from a lender who just wants to offload it. This is why lenders prefer to keep working with you to achieve an acceptable resolution.

However, you must also bear in mind in any negotiations that the lender by its nature is not likely to hold on to property, and therefore, at some point, if they cannot achieve a resolution, they will take the option of selling, even if this means that they take a loss. This is also why a restructuring of debt or debt forgiveness is possible.

However, do not assume that all of the cards are in your hands. You need to remember that your liability is not the value of the house but the amount of the loan. Any breakdown in the negotiations with your lender that leads to a legal process will add cost to your loan, which may or may not be recoverable by the lender. You will also incur legal costs if you decide to fight your case in court.

As the amount of your liability is the borrowings, it is in your interest to try to avoid a situation that reduces the value of the property or increases the amount that you owe your lender. In the unlikely event of a property sale, you may still owe a residual amount because the loan is not fully cleared. The payment or otherwise of this will be subject to further negotiation.

Mutual Agreement Is the Best Option

It is clear from what we have just outlined that reaching a mutual and acceptable agreement is the best way forward. You should also realise that there is a lot in your favour and that the lender will be seeking an amicable result.

You also now know that the process – from the day you find yourself in difficulties to finally losing your home – is a long one. It is a long process because your lender will want to exhaust all avenues for a solution. For your part, it is important that you remain in negotiations and engage with the lender.

To achieve the best result you must do your homework well, understand your financial position, be prepared to present your case and stay calm and confident that you can achieve the result.

Time Is on Your Side

In relation to house repossessions, your lender is required to make every reasonable attempt to agree an alternative arrangement with you or your nominated representative before applying to the court to commence legal action for repossession.

The significance of co-operating with your lender cannot be overstated. *Do not ignore the problem, and do not ignore your lender.* Once you are co-operating with your lender they must wait at least twelve months from the day you were classified as in need of the resolution process before applying to the courts to commence legal action.

This twelve-month period excludes any time that you are complying with any alternative arrangement agreed with your lender, any time you were in an appeals process, or any time you spent considering entering into an appeals process. So, the underlying point here is, there is a significant amount of time allotted to you where the lender cannot make a move to repossess your house, and this time can be used productively to do an acceptable deal and also to deal with your financial position.

PIAs: The Solution for Secured Debt

The new insolvency legislation provides three new processes, two of which deal with unsecured debt and were covered in Chapter 13. We shall now look at PIAs, the solution for secured debt or, more specifically, family homes and buy-to-let properties.

PIAs apply to secured debt up to €3,000,000. They allow a debtor to pay a portion of what is due to creditors over six years (with a possible extension to seven years) and then be discharged from further liability. Achieving this solution is not as easy as it looks: there are eligibility criteria and rules, and your lender must agreed to any proposed solution. However, PIAs may be worth exploring as part of your strategy to solve your financial difficulties.

The first thing to know about PIAs is that, while they are negotiated directly with your lender, you do not do the negotiation. The process has a set procedure and timeline, and you need to engage a personal insolvency practitioner to negotiate and administer the process on your behalf.

The personal insolvency practitioner will assess your eligibility for a PIA, and there are a number of key drivers that will allow you to enter this process. If you are successful, the PIA facilitates an arrangement under which you pay your creditors, such as your lender, a portion of what is due to them over a six- or seven-year period and are then discharged from further liability as outlined in the agreement.

Key elements of the PIA process include the following:

- You must be insolvent.
- The process covers both secured and unsecured debts.
- A PIA only covers secured debt up to €3,000,000, unless all secured creditors agree to allow secured debt above this to be included.
- Preferential creditors such as the Revenue Commissioners have to be paid in full unless they agree otherwise.
- Your personal insolvency practitioner must issue a certificate to the effect that in his/her opinion there is no likelihood of your becoming solvent within a five-year period.
- A statement of your assets and liabilities must be sworn.

- The process cannot include a requirement where you cease to occupy or dispose of your principal private residence.
- The proposal must provide for a reasonable living for you and your dependants.
- You must qualify under resident or domicile rules as being resident in Ireland.

Prior Engagement with Your Lender

You must also have shown positive engagement with your secured creditors in the period leading up to an application. In relation to mortgage arrears on your principal private residence, you will be required to make a statutory declaration that you have co-operated with your secured creditors for at least six months before the application.

You can only avail of the PIA once, which is why you need to be fully involved in the solution to your financial difficulties from the start. If you agree a deal you must be able to stick to it. When it comes to personal insolvency there is no second chance. Failure to agree on the PIA leaves open the option of debt enforcement by judicial bankruptcy. For the principal private residence, the protections afforded under MARP continue to be available to co-operating borrowers.

Do the lenders have a veto on whether I get the arrangement?

In order to successfully achieve a PIA you must get the agreement of your lender and other creditors, who will vote on the arrangement proposed by your personal insolvency practitioner. The legislation provides for a voting structure between your creditors which requires a majority approval. Your insolvency practitioner will handle the exact legal requirements, but, in general, to achieve agreement to your proposal you need the following:

- The majority of creditors (representing 65 per cent in value) who are participating and voting
- Among your creditors there may be those who are secured on some assets and those who have no security for the amount owed (unsecured), so there is a further voting threshold:
  - 50 per cent of the value of secured debts due to creditors who are entitled to vote and have voted at the meeting as secured creditors
  - 50 per cent of the value of unsecured debts due to creditors who are entitled to vote and have voted at the meeting as unsecured creditors

In deciding whether your lender or any other creditor has a veto you must consider their voting power in their category of debt. Part of the role of your insolvency practitioner is to assess this, talk to your creditors and structure a deal that is acceptable to both you and your lenders.

How do you get into a PIA?

A PIA is only available where the debts owed to secured debtors are less than €3,000,000. For secured debt above this you must get the agreement of all secured creditors to include them. If you have secured debt over €3,000,000 and your creditors do not agree to this being included you will have to negotiate directly with your lenders or perhaps look at the bankruptcy route (see Chapter 15).

In order to enter a PIA you must provide sworn details of your assets and liabilities. It is likely that a financial statement similar to the standard financial statement for the mortgage arrears process will be required. The difference here is that a financial statement for personal insolvency is a sworn document. If it is later discovered that you concealed any assets it could render your agreement void and send you back to where you started.

You must engage the services of a personal insolvency practitioner, to whom you provide the sworn statement of assets and liabilities. The insolvency practitioner will take you through the legal requirements and assess your eligibility. An initial consultation with a qualified and experienced insolvency practitioner early in your negotiations with your lender may be advisable, as it will establish whether you could be eligible and what options are available.

What is the role of the personal insolvency practitioner?

The personal insolvency practitioner has many duties to carry out in order to achieve a successful result. The first things they can do for you are:

- Get you a protective certificate, which will give you protection from your creditors/lenders for a period of 70 days (which can be extended by 40 days)
- During this protection period, seek to achieve an agreed solution to your debt problem which will involve debt forgiveness
- Liaise with the Insolvency Service in relation to their requirements

The personal insolvency practitioner will request your financial statement of assets, liabilities and expenditure so that they can assess your eligibility for a PIA.

Based on the criteria set out in the legislation and your financial position, if they are happy that you are eligible they will apply to the Insolvency Service of Ireland for a protective certificate. If they are satisfied, it will show the court that the application for a protective certificate is in order. If the court is satisfied that you meet the prescribed criteria, it must issue a protective certificate.

The protective certificate gives you protection from your creditors (in other words, they cannot take action) for 70 days, which may be extended for a further 40 days if good progress on a solution is made.

There are at present many practitioners in the marketplace who are ready to assist with personal insolvency, and the number is likely to increase. As personal insolvency is not a judicial process, many professionals can get involved in this work. There may be a new form of registration or authorisation for this role (as for financial advisers), and it is important that you work with someone who is authorised and qualified to represent you to your lenders.

Once the protection certificate is obtained, the process of seeking agreement with your lender and other creditors on a solution to your financial difficulties, as outlined in the table below, begins.

The Personal Insolvency Process

Person or Agency	Action
You	You have exhausted your discussions with your lender on your debt, gone through the MARP process and are unsure whether you are achieving a result that fits your financial circumstances. You decide to explore the option of entering a PIA and arrange a meeting with a qualified and experienced professional in this area who is registered to practise as a personal insolvency practitioner.
Personal Insolvency Practitioner	Your personal insolvency practitioner reviews your financial statement. If they are happy that you fulfil the criteria, they will apply to the court, through the Insolvency Service of Ireland, for a protection certificate.

(Continued)

The Personal Insolvency Process (*Continued*)

Person or Agency	Action
Insolvency Service and Court	If the court is satisfied that you meet the criteria, it will issue the protection certificate following an approach from the Insolvency Service of Ireland.
Protection Certificate	The protection certificate provides an initial 70 days' protection from creditors and may be extended by a further 40 days on application.
Lenders and Other Creditors	During this protection period, creditors' actions against you are prohibited.
Personal Insolvency Practitioner	During this protection period, your personal insolvency practitioner interacts with your lenders and creditors and seeks to formulate an agreed personal insolvency arrangement.
Lenders and Other Creditors	At a meeting arranged by your personal insolvency practitioner, your lenders and other creditors vote on the proposal for dealing with your debt put forward by your personal insolvency practitioner.
Lenders and Other Creditors	If the proposal is agreed, any individual creditor has 21 days to object.
Court	If there are no valid objections, the court confirms the arrangement if it is satisfied that it is compliant. This confirmation binds all the creditors to the arrangement.
Personal Insolvency Practitioner	Your personal insolvency practitioner stays involved for the six to seven years' duration of the arrangement.

Secured Creditors

Secured creditors are prohibited from taking steps to release their security. This may not include secured creditors holding security other than real property; for example, shares or other tradeable investments. A party prejudiced by the granting of the protective certificate can apply to have it set aside on the grounds of unfair prejudice to that creditor.

Guarantors

All parties to the borrowing must be kept informed and involved in the discussions. This may be the only way they can seek to agree an acceptable deal for themselves.

The protective certificate issued by the court only protects you – it does not prohibit a secured creditor from taking action against a guarantor.

Case Study

Enda has secured debts of less than €3,000,000, which are guaranteed by his father, Thomas. Enda engages the services of a personal insolvency practitioner who successfully secures a protection certificate for him.

Enda has 70 days' (with a possible further 40 days') protection from creditors, during which his personal insolvency practitioner will seek to put together a personal insolvency arrangement.

Thomas is not covered by the protection certificate and can still be pursued as guarantor by Enda's creditors.

This could prove a problem for many people who, on a personal level, could benefit from the insolvency legislation but who have gained the loan from their lender on foot of a parental guarantee. Their options may be restricted to the mortgage arrears process in order to avoid triggering a move by their lender against the guarantor.

You Get to Stay in the Family Home

As with the mortgage arrears process, there is a strong emphasis on keeping people in their family home. Accordingly, the PIA cannot require you to sell your principal private residence unless either:

- You agree to do so – you cannot be compelled to sell.
- The personal insolvency practitioner forms the option that the costs of staying in the home are disproportionately larger – he or she must then agree with you that this is the best option.

However, you must remember that to achieve a good result under a PIA you must get the agreement of 65 per cent in value of your creditors and 50 per cent of secured creditors. Bear in mind that should your application fail and the next option is bankruptcy, the house will be sold under that process – in bankruptcy all assets are sold.

Both MARP and the personal insolvency process strongly favour keeping people in their home, and it is implied in the codes and legislation that both borrowers and creditors will work hard to achieve an agreed result.

In fact the amendment to the Bankruptcy Act discourages the use of bankruptcy before all other avenues are exhausted. The court is permitted to adjourn bankruptcy proceedings if it takes the view that a debtor's situation could be better dealt with by the insolvency legislation.

However, in relation to achieving an agreement with lenders, the family home may prove the biggest difficulty. The idea of forgiving debt after a six- or seven-year period and allowing an individual to stay in a prestigious home will be hard fought, as your lender may look for trading down as part of the solution.

Maintaining Your Standard of Living

If you enter a PIA, what impact will it have on your living standards? As already discussed in Chapter 12, the Personal Insolvency Act 2012 states:

> ... a Personal Insolvency Arrangement should not contain any terms which would require the debtor to make payments of such an amount that the debtor would not have sufficient income to maintain a reasonable standard of living for the debtor and his/her dependants.

However, 'reasonable standard of living' is not defined and may cause difficulties for lenders and borrowers. The Insolvency Service is due to give guidance on this; however, different people have different ideas of what constitutes a reasonable standard of living.

Financial Statements

One of the eligibility criteria is the requirement to complete financial statements and make a statutory declaration confirming that the statement is a complete and accurate statement of your assets, liabilities and income and expenditure.

What happens next?

Once the PIA is agreed and approved by the court, it will be subject to review at least every twelve months, and a new statement will be completed for each review, which is circulated to your creditors. If there is a positive change in your circumstances, payments to your lenders and other creditors can be increased. However, it seems from the legislation that only 50 per cent of any new assets acquired by you would be made available to your creditors.

What happens when the PIA ends?

When the term of the PIA ends, after six or seven years, all your unsecured debts stand discharged, but the secured debts are not discharged unless that is specified in the terms of the arrangement. The key to relief from your secured creditors will be to get them to write down the loans under the agreement to either the current value of their security or a level that you can afford to pay off over time.

The legislation dictates that the principal owed to a secured creditor cannot be written down to less than the value of their security. It also provides for a claw-back in the event of a subsequent sale of a mortgaged property at a higher level than the mortgage has been written down.

How might I fare under a PIA?

There are lots of good aspects to a PIA: the emphasis on you remaining in your home, having a reasonable lifestyle and achieving debt forgiveness. Achieving these benefits relies on your personal insolvency practitioner being able to construct an arrangement that will be accepted by your lenders and other creditors. Any arrangement will need to provide benefits to you and your creditors, so it is worth considering what these might be.

For you, benefits might include:

- Adequate level of debt forgiveness
- Acceptable living standard during the process and an improvement thereafter
- Long-term agreement on a debt level which is serviceable
- Retention of the family home

For your lenders and creditors, benefits might include:

- Maximum possible recovery of debt
- Sale of family home if considered excessive in size and value

- Lifestyle restrained to modest needs to maximise loan repayments
- Receipt of payments beyond the six/seven years of the agreement
- Minimal debt forgiveness

Is a deal possible if both sides seem so far apart? Well, the answer to this depends on the relative power of the negotiating parties and the flexibility of each to achieve a result. Most negotiations have an element of trade-off. These are benefits that one party is willing to trade to gain more of something else. If we look at the benefits (or demands) of each party in the above lists there are some trade-offs:

- If your lender forces the sale of the house would you be better off with bankruptcy?
- If you go to bankruptcy your lender may forego the opportunity to get continuing payments after the personal insolvency period is over in six or seven years.
- If you accept and can live with more debt, staying in your current home may be more palatable to the lender.

You can see now that the possibilities are many. This is why the legislation makes it mandatory that you use a personal insolvency practitioner. The deal may hinge on the following factors:

- What assets can be sold now to reduce debt?
- How much debt can you service going forward from your income? It is unlikely that lenders will go below this amount.
- What are your prospects for greater earnings in the future? If positive, can a portion of the debt be warehoused until things improve?
- Is your current family home too large for your altered circumstances? Is trading down to a smaller home feasible?

- Does your profession allow you to continue working if you are made bankrupt?
- How will your creditors fare if you are made bankrupt?

Case Study

Mark and Jenny are joint borrowers on their family home, three buy-to-let properties and a holiday home.

Mark is a professional who earned substantial income during the boom, which he invested in property and moving to a new home. His income is now much lower, but the couple would still be very comfortable if they did not have debt of €2,900,000, which is currently on a capital and interest basis over 25 years.

All the properties have fallen in value and their current position is as follows:

Property	Historic Value	Current Value	Debt Level
Family home	€2,500,000	€900,000	€1,200,000
Investment properties	€1,500,000	€800,000	€1,500,000
Holiday home	€500,000	€300,000	€200,000
Total	**€4,500,000**	**€2,000,000**	**€2,900,000**

Based on this, Mark and Jenny need to consider the following:

- Debt servicing of the €2,900,000 over 25 years amounts to €183,000 per year.
- Interest servicing at 4 per cent is €116,000.
- Mark and his personal insolvency practitioner work out that he can service debt of €1,200,000 on current and prospective earnings over 25 years. This amounts to €6,300 per month or €76,000 per year.
- Mark wants to hold on to his house and needs to structure a deal that achieves this goal. His family would like to

> retain the holiday home, which has been in the family for many years and was an inheritance from Jenny's parents.
> • Bankruptcy would impact Michael's professional status, so this is not an option.

This example shows the choices that have to be faced. A sale of all assets would return €2,000,000 to the creditors. Mark and Jenny could rent a property for, say, €2,500 per month and repay the balance of the loans amounting to €900,000 over 25 years. This would probably suit the lenders as they would get an immediate debt reduction.

However, Mark and Jenny can service €1,200,000 in debt and the home loan is €1,200,000. As long as Mark is paying his home loan it may be difficult for the lenders to force a sale of this property. He is unable to service the debt on the holiday home. Mark could decide to sell the investment properties and the holiday home, realising €1,100,000, and look to have his lenders warehouse the €600,000 until things improve.

If Mark and Jenny have multiple lenders they would have to consider the relative strength and security position of the lenders and what options are open to them. If, for example, the lenders on the investment properties are different from the lenders on the family property, they will recover little from making Mark and Jenny bankrupt as the home is in negative equity. They would also cut off Mark's earning capability.

The example of Mark and Jenny serves to highlight that nothing is straightforward and constructing an acceptable outcome will take skill, patience and negotiation.

What about the cost of entering a PIA?

The legislation states that provision for cost and outlay be provided for in the PIA. It seems that any payment to creditors will be after provision for costs.

What if I do not stick to the terms of the PIA?

If you fail to meet your obligation under the arrangement for more than six months, the arrangement is terminated, and all debts covered by the arrangement are reinstated unless the court orders differently. The lesson here is to ensure you can live up to the agreement before you agree to it and then to make sure that you do stick to it. Also bear in mind that you can only have one PIA in your lifetime. Unlike the mortgage arrears process, if it breaks down, you may be able to do a new deal. The personal insolvency legislation only gives you one opportunity.

SUMMARY

We now have a personal insolvency process that puts debt forgiveness firmly on the agenda and seeks the resolution of your personal debt difficulties in that context. The insolvency process is focused and time-critical and involves court oversight. No party to the process can be complacent. The key to success will be to convince your lenders that their best alternative solution, which in some cases may involve bankruptcy, is significantly less than your offer.

The process lasts six or seven years, during which time you will experience a modest living standard and may get to stay in your current house, if not required to trade down. If you comply with the terms you will be relieved of unsecured debt at the end of the process. Secure debt remains in place, but the key is to negotiate it down to an acceptable level.

Key Points in this Chapter

1. A non-judicial process has now been put in place to deal with personal debt and insolvency.
2. There are three new processes: Debt Relief Notices (DRNs), Debt Settlement Arrangements (DSAs) and Personal Insolvency Arrangements (PIAs).
3. PIAs will be of most interest to people with secured mortgage debt under €3,000,000.
4. You will have to engage a personal insolvency practitioner to represent you to your lenders. Under this process you are not allowed to deal directly with your lenders.
5. You will have to prove eligibility under the criteria set down, and these will be assessed by your personal insolvency practitioner.
6. Being insolvent and projected to remain that way for the next five years are key eligibility criteria, but there are others.
7. Retaining a family home, even your current one, is a distinct possibility and is emphasised in the legislation.
8. You will also be allowed a reasonable standard of living.
9. You can only have one PIA in your lifetime, and if you breach it you could be back to where you started.
10. This is a process worth considering, at least initially, with your adviser.

15

Is Bankruptcy an Option?

Let us never negotiate out of fear. But let us never fear to negotiate.
John F. Kennedy, US President, 1961–1963

So you have followed all the procedures we have discussed in this book. You have made an accurate assessment of your living expenses and full disclosure of your assets and liabilities; you entered into the mortgage arrears process and your lender has now made an assessment and offered you a deal. That deal was provided in writing, but it was not acceptable to you.

Your next step is to look at personal insolvency, and if you do not get a result there you may have to consider bankruptcy. It is important to consider this option well in advance – and before you seek a PIA – so be sure to put it on the agenda with your personal insolvency practitioner. Most insolvency practitioners will be knowledgeable about bankruptcy and will be able to assess its impact on you and whether it is a viable option; however, it may be worth checking that they do have this knowledge, as there may be many new entrants to the insolvency space in the coming months.

In fact, if things are not going your way under the mortgage arrears process at the lower levels, where debt deferment is the most likely option, it is worth arranging a meeting with an insolvency practitioner and reviewing the following:

- Your eligibility for a PIA and the possible outcome
- An assessment of bankruptcy as an option for you

Knowing where you stand in relation to both these processes will temper your approach to negotiations on your personal debt. For instance, if bankruptcy is not an option that you can consider, the proposal you put to your lenders as part of a PIA will have to be significantly better than your lenders and other creditors could expect if they made you bankrupt.

Should your lender vote against the proposal put forward by your personal insolvency practitioner, they may not move quickly to bankruptcy. They may just wait and see whether you propose another option or whether you agree with their proposal. This is most likely to be the case if they are secured and see no reason to rush; however, their attitude may change if they feel their security is at risk.

One of the main reasons they may delay is the cost of bankruptcy proceedings. The cost of the court-appointed official assignee and the petitioning creditors' costs must be discharged before any payment is made to creditors. A lender has to be sure that the money spent on the process and the ongoing cost of running the bankruptcy is recoverable and that the funds left over will return a sufficient amount of the moneys lent. In some cases your lender may ignore these costs, if they are frustrated in finding another acceptable solution and see it as the only course of action.

I do not propose to go into the legal intricacies of bankruptcy in this book – this is best left to your insolvency practitioner – but I will give you a flavour of what is involved and allow you to consider it as part of your overall strategy in dealing with debt. It will be helpful to understand the general process and outcome. With this knowledge you will be better placed to negotiate with your lender. Remember, you will need to take specific advice on your particular circumstances should you wish to consider this route – that is, if you cannot come to a better solution with your lender or lenders.

The idea of bankruptcy strikes terror into many people's hearts. An attempt to avoid bankruptcy may lead them to consider options that may have a more long-term detrimental impact on their financial life. We conjure up visions of debtor's prison, a life of hardship and, perhaps most important, the social stigma and disgrace that many people associate with bankruptcy. However, since personal insolvency and even bankruptcy will become more common in the coming years, the social aspect may in turn become less relevant. It is also worth noting that those people who view their debt problem as a business-related outcome are less reticent to consider bankruptcy or (in the case of companies) liquidation as the solution.

In the past, due to the draconian nature of the legislation in Ireland, bankruptcy was viewed as something to be avoided at all costs. Perhaps the worst element of it was the length of time – twelve years – you remained a bankrupt. In many countries this is not the case; for example in the UK it is just one year. The legislation recently enacted has set the time at three years, which may make it a more palatable option that deserves close consideration, particularly for certain people.

Professionals who rely on a certification from the association for their profession, or where there is a legal bar on them practising their profession if they are made bankrupt, may find it less attractive. However, if you have unsustainable debt, the reduction of the bankruptcy period to three years means that you cannot ignore it when framing your approach to dealing with financial difficulties.

Another thing to consider is that any negotiation with your lenders and creditors that seems to restrict your options will make it less likely that you can get an acceptable deal.

Case Study

Martina is seeking to negotiate a debt settlement with her lenders. She has looked at all options and, after reviewing the figures, she and her financial adviser believe that making a fresh start using the bankruptcy laws is a real option.

However, Martina is initially trying to achieve a deal with her lenders that will provide a reasonable level of debt reduction and maintain a lifestyle that will keep her family happy while she gets back on her feet.

She believes she has a trump card in being able to go the bankruptcy route, but after discussing this option with her family she has been given the following conditions:

- Selling investment properties is acceptable, but they do not want to give up the family home.
- They wish to continue in private schools and retain their current lifestyle.
- Selling overseas property is not fully supported.

You can see that Martina's negotiating position with her lender is much reduced, as her threat of going all the way to bankruptcy may not be believed, and she will not, in any case, be able to achieve this due to her family's demands.

Doing the deal with your lender is like any negotiation: the more you care about achieving a particular outcome – and the clearer that becomes to the other side – the more you will have to give up. Meeting your lender and saying that everything is negotiable but you want to remain in your house leaves you at a disadvantage. You should look at all options and then assess their impact on your lifestyle and on all those affected. Your first major negotiation will be with yourself and those affected by the result you seek to achieve.

Is Bankruptcy a Real Option?

In the past, borrowers viewed bankruptcy as a significant threat to their financial position and lifestyle. This tended to motivate them to do a deal with their lender. The threat is less stark now, particularly as in many cases high unsustainable debt levels make the alternative no less stark. Which is better, a life tied to an unsustainable debt burden or three years in bankruptcy? The revised rules may change people's attitude to this route if the hoped-for solutions under the insolvency legislation do not materialise.

Also, as touched on earlier, business people who either have significant debt in their own name or are affected by personal guarantees for company debt may view bankruptcy as a fresh start and have no real difficulty viewing it as a solution.

It may also become the case that as more people use the insolvency and bankruptcy route to solve their debt problem the reluctance of others will subside, particularly if those close to them are successful at achieving debt forgiveness in the process. Lenders may have to be careful in over-using any perceived veto they have, as we may reach a tipping point at which insolvency and bankruptcy become more commonplace out of lack of progress on the other solutions. Lenders that take a flexible and innovative approach to the long-term mortgage arrears solutions may achieve the best result for themselves and an acceptable one for borrowers.

Asset Sales

Bankruptcy is a formal court process which you can commence yourself. Alternatively, one of your creditors can petition to make you bankrupt. While bankruptcy is normally considered to arise where a person is insolvent, there are in fact a number of acts of bankruptcy that can result in someone being adjudicated bankrupt. These tend to involve property or other asset transactions that show evidence of intent to deprive creditors of these assets. The Bankruptcy Act is more specific on these and it may be worth reviewing them with your adviser. In this chapter, though, we will focus on bankruptcy as a solution to insolvency.

However, as I will explain, if you are happy to enter this process it may be best from a cost point of view to leave it to one of your creditors to petition for your bankruptcy. Any creditor owed €20,000 or more can petition for your bankruptcy. The recent amendments to the Bankruptcy Act raised the level of debt required for a person to petition for bankruptcy to €20,000 (from €1,900), so smaller claims are excluded, though there is provision for joint applications totalling €20,000.

If your lender or other creditor successfully petitions for your bankruptcy and a bankruptcy order is issued, your assets fall under the control of a court-appointed official assignee. The official assignee becomes responsible for uncovering as much as possible about your assets and liabilities and maximising the amount returned to your creditors, within certain guidelines.

The official assignee deals with all practical aspects of the day-to-day running of the bankruptcy, such as disposing of your assets and certifying to the High Court who the creditors are for the purpose of Irish bankruptcy law.

You will be required to disclose all property to the court and to deliver all your property to the official assignee. There are criminal sanctions in the Act for failure to co-operate with the court in the administration of your estate.

Do I get protection from my creditors?

As with personal insolvency, once a bankruptcy order has been made, your creditors can no longer pursue you for payment. All uncompleted legal enforcements against you are stopped. The idea is that all your creditors will be treated equally. However, secured creditors can realise their security separately from bankruptcy. Secured creditors, such as your lenders, have a number of options when their security is insufficient to repay the loan in order to recover the unsecured amount in the bankruptcy. These can be outlined by your insolvency practitioner. The core point is that, as is the case under the insolvency procedure, creditors cease to interact with you and all dealings will be with the official assignee. This will provide some relief from the stress of your financial difficulties.

Can I keep my job?

Your employment may be affected. Certain professionals are barred from practising if they are made bankrupt. You cannot act as a director or take part in the management of a company. If you are in employment, your salary is likely to be attached in favour of the official assignee, and any property or assets you acquire subsequent to adjudication must be handed over to the official assignee. So there seems to be no bar on working – subject to the constraints mentioned.

Another restriction that is placed on you in bankruptcy is your ability to obtain credit and thereby continue in business. You cannot obtain credit over €1,000 without disclosing your bankruptcy status. The Act does provide that you can retain the tools of your trade and some other items to the value of €6,000.

Do I lose the family home?

The assets that can be appropriated include your family home. The assignee must apply to the High Court to permit the sale of the family home. Normally a court will take into account the requirements and financial resources of the spouse and children and has the discretion to postpone a sale; however, the interests of the lenders and other creditors take priority at the end of the day.

It may be best to assume that your family home will be sold to pay creditors. Your spouse or other co-owners may have an entitlement to part of the proceeds if there is equity in the house and they are not party to the debts or they are not made bankrupt. This is complex and needs specific analysis with your adviser. If you are made bankrupt it is your assets that are sold, but if your spouse or partner is party to all the lending, they may also be made bankrupt.

What kind of living standard will we have?

If you are employed, the court can make an order for you to make payments to the official assignee from your salary. However, in making the order, the court is required to provide for reasonable living expenses for you and your family when making any ongoing payment. You will be allowed a reasonable standard of living, but whether you find this acceptable for your needs is another question. Under the amendments to the Bankruptcy Act, while the time period for bankruptcy has been reduced from twelve to three years, there is provision for continued payments for a further five years following discharge, under certain circumstances.

When will I be freed from bankruptcy?

Under the new amendments to the Bankruptcy Act, automatic discharge from bankruptcy will be possible after three years (as opposed to twelve) and in a sense this is what makes bankruptcy a more attractive option now, particularly for those with a severe debt problem and who can see no light at the end of the tunnel. No matter what the restrictions are, you are free of your debts after three years, and if you have the skill and ability you can achieve a fresh start.

You will remain liable for certain debts, such as fines, debts arising from family proceedings, etc.

Is bankruptcy an attractive option?

Bankruptcy is a very complex procedure and is not easy to explain. I hope the above gives you food for thought. Certainly some of the results of bankruptcy seemed harsh and uninviting when the process lasted twelve years. However, now that the term has been reduced to three years, many of the items outlined above will seem less harsh, particularly when weighed against a lifetime of unsustainable debt. As I have already stated, bankruptcy and its effects are personal to you and sound professional advice is required, but it should not be ruled out too soon if your negotiations with your lender are not achieving the desired result.

Amendments to the Bankruptcy Act

Your lender may be wary of the recent amendments to the Bankruptcy Act. The use of bankruptcy as a method of solving the personal debt problem is discouraged under the new legislation. It permits the court to adjourn bankruptcy proceedings if the court takes the view that your situation could best be dealt with by a DSA or PIA.

The awarding of costs to the petitioner (the person seeking your bankruptcy) is now discretionary, whereas in the past it was automatic. It is also conditional on the court's view of the reasonableness of the behaviour of the petitioning lender or other creditors with regard to any refusal to accept a DSA or PIA.

It also increases the period for which transactions undertaken by the bankrupt person can be examined from three months to three years, and any transaction deemed fraudulent may be reversed.

SUMMARY

The new amendments will make your lender think before moving to making you bankrupt, as they cannot be certain that their costs will be covered. The case could be referred back to seek a PIA. Accordingly, using each step of the four levels (discussed in Parts II and III of this book) makes sense while you build your case for interest forgiveness or debt forgiveness. Knowing your financial information and staying engaged are also paramount so that you can prove that you engaged with your lenders on a reasonable basis.

Constructing a proposal that provides a better outcome for your lender and other creditors than can be achieved through bankruptcy will stand the best chance of achieving a result that avoids this final step.

Bankruptcy is a complex area and the working assumption should be that all your assets, including your family home, will be sold. Assets that remain with the family but are not the property of the bankrupt person are not included in the bankruptcy, but there is now a provision to look at transactions that took place over the previous three years to see whether they can be reversed.

The shorter timeframe of three years makes bankruptcy an option for consideration by those who are not dependent on a professional certification to carry out their work.

As with all the processes for dealing with your financial difficulties, individual advice is necessary – your case is unique to you.

Key Points in this Chapter

1. Recently there have been major changes to the bankruptcy laws, possibly the most significant of which is the reduction – from twelve years to three years – of the period after which a bankrupt will be discharged from bankruptcy.

---

2. The changes also discourage the use of bankruptcy by both your creditors and you in favour of fully exploring the options under the insolvency legislation.
3. Awarding of costs, which was previously automatic for the petitioner, is now discretionary, so, should your lender or other creditor petition for your bankruptcy, they will not be certain of getting their costs.
4. Asset sales and other transfers in the last three years can now be scrutinised and if deemed fraudulent may be reversed. Previously this period was three months, so this is a big change in favour of creditors.
5. The provision of a reasonable living standard for you and your dependants has been introduced and, subject to guidelines expected from the Insolvency Service of Ireland, may provide a better standard of living than normally expected under bankruptcy.
6. The sale of your family home is more than likely, so you should consider this option carefully.
7. For professionals who are barred from practising if made bankrupt, this option may not be available. Therefore they may need to rely on the insolvency legislation.
8. For entrepreneurs looking for a fresh start bankruptcy is now a better option than it was in the past.
9. Bankruptcy will impact on your ability to attract credit in the future: however, all the arrears processes discussed in this book will affect your credit rating.
10. Bankruptcy is complex. It requires a lot of consideration and professional advice before entering it and using it as an option to resolve your debt problem.

Useful Websites

Fran Dalton – www.francisdalton.com or francisdalton. com/blog
You will get some more information on my website, and I cover general queries on my blog.

National Consumer Agency – www.nca.ie
The National Consumer Agency (NCA) is a statutory body established by the Irish Government in May 2007 to enforce consumer law and promote consumer rights.

There is much good advice on this site, including how to use your money, some financial calculators and advice on how to make a complaint about a financial services provider. You can contact the NCA on their website or through the consumer helpline on 1890 432432.

Central Bank of Ireland – www.centralbank.ie
You will find the Code of Conduct on Mortgage Arrears and other codes discussed under the Financial Regulation tab of the Central Bank website. For general enquiries regarding financial sector regulations you can contact the Central Bank at 1890 777777 or online at enquiries@centralbank.ie.

Irish Statute Book – www.irishstatutebook.ie
The electronic Irish Statute Book database includes Acts of the Oireachtas and Statutory Instruments (secondary legislation). You can view the Personal Insolvency Act 2012 on this

site. You can also access information regarding the Bankruptcy Act 1988 on the site.

Mortgage Advice and Budgeting Service (MABS) – www. mabs.ie
MABS is the only free, independent and confidential service for people in debt or going into debt in Ireland. If you are in debt and have many lenders and other creditors MABS can review your situation and put a proposal to them on your behalf. The organisation has a helpline that can be reached on 0761 072000 or, alternatively, they can be contacted online at helpline@mabs.ie.

Citizens Information – www.citizensinformation.ie
Citizens Information provides information on public services and entitlements in Ireland. It is provided by the Citizens Information Board. You can contact the information service by phoning the Citizens Information Phone Service on 0761 074000 or by visiting your local Citizens Information Centre.

Keep Your Home – www.keepyourhome.ie
This website is provided by the Citizens Information Board and the Money Advice and Budgeting Service (MABS). It provides information on services and entitlements if you are having difficulty paying your rent or making your mortgage repayments. It also provides a Mortgage Arrears Information Helpline, on 0761 074050.

Irish Society of Insolvency Practitioners – www.isip.ie
The ISIP was set up in 2004, and its members include people from some of the most successful accounting and legal firms in the country. If you are looking for an experienced personal insolvency practitioner the ISIP should be able to guide you. You can contact the ISIP through their website.

Your Lender's Website
Your bank will have a copy of the Standard Financial Statement on its website as well as details of its process for handling mortgage arrears.

Newspapers and Media Outlets
It is a good idea to stay informed of developments in the mortgage crisis by keeping up to date with current affairs. Review the websites of all major media outlets as they will report on any deals with or changing attitudes of the banks. This may guide your own efforts in achieving what you require.